THE SPIRITUAL WARRIOR'S PRAYER GUIDE

The Spiritual Warrior's Prayer Guide

Quin Sherrer
and
Ruthanne Garlock

... My word that goes out from my mouth:
It will not return to me empty,
but will accomplish what I desire
and achieve the purpose for which I sent it.
Isaiah 55:11

Servant Publications
Ann Arbor, Michigan

Vine Books is an imprint of Servant Publications especially designed
to serve Evangelical Christians.

Scripture quoted by permission. All quotations unless otherwise indicated
are from *THE HOLY BIBLE: NEW INTERNATIONAL VERSION*®. Copyright
© 1973, 1978, 1983 International Bible Society. Used by permission of
Zondervan Publishing House. All rights reserved.

The "NIV" and "New International Version" trademarks are registered in
the United States Patent and Trademark Office by International Bible
Society.

Other versions quoted are abbreviated as follows: AMP, *The Amplified Bible*,
Old Testament copyright © 1965, 1987 by the Zondervan Corporation and
The Amplified New Testament copyright © 1958, 1987 by the Lockman
Foundation, used by permission; NKJV, *New King James Version*, copyright ©
1979, 1980, 1982 by Thomas Nelson Inc., Publishers, used by permission;
TLB, *The Living Bible*, © 1971 by Tyndale House Publishers, used by permis-
sion; NASB, *New American Standard Bible*, copyright © 1960, 1962, 1963,
1968, 1971, 1972, 1973, 1975, 1977 by the Lockman Foundation, used by
permission; KJV, *King James Version*, the Authorized Version, Zondervan
Publishing House, used by permission.

Published by Servant Publications
P.O. Box 8617
Ann Arbor, MI 48107

Cover design by Michael Andaloro

95 96 10 9 8 7 6

Printed in the United States of America.

ISBN 0-89283-809-4

Library of Congress Cataloging-in-Publication Data

Sherrer, Quin.
   The spiritual warrior's prayer guide / Quin Sherrer and
Ruthanne Garlock.
       p.   cm.
Includes bibliographical references.
ISBN 0-89283-809-4
1. Spiritual warfare—Prayer-books and devotions—English.
I. Garlock, Ruthanne. II. Title.
BV4509.5.S47   1992
248.3'2—dc20   92-22920

OTHER BOOKS BY THE AUTHORS

How to Pray for Your Children
by
Quin Sherrer

How to Forgive Your Children
How to Pray for Your Family and Friends
A Woman's Guide to Spiritual Warfare
by
Quin Sherrer and Ruthanne Garlock

Before We Kill and Eat You
Fire in His Bones
by
Ruthanne Garlock

Contents

Introduction

THE APOSTLE PAUL challenges believers to oppose the powers of darkness while standing in God's strength and armor, and to "pray in the Spirit on all occasions with all kinds of prayers...." We cannot afford to remain passive in the face of these foes. Here are just a few examples of the many readers who have written us asking for help in spiritual warfare. As you can see, some almost feel overwhelmed by those powers of darkness.

- A young woman sexually abused by her stepfather (a pastor) from age seven to thirteen forgave him before he died, but still struggles to forgive her mother who allowed the abuse.
- A wife whose Muslim husband has now accepted the Lord asks us to pray that they will be able to learn about spiritual warfare, then move to the Middle East to witness to his family.
- A mother requests prayer ammunition to fight for the deliverance of her sixteen-year-old son, who has been dabbling in the occult and been diagnosed as manic depressive.
- A wife being beaten by her husband while they have sex; he has even deformed her. "People think my husband is a good man, but he's not a friend to Jesus.... Soon the Lord will free me or bring my husband to salvation."

- A pastor concerned that Satan has so blinded believers that most live spiritually unproductive lives.
- An immigrant from Europe wanting to find a church that believes in prayer and spiritual warfare. "I have no friend or prayer partner to help me."
- A teenager wanting to follow Jesus, but struggling. "I'm beginning to understand what kind of a war we really are in. Satan tries to confuse me and blind me, and tells me I'll fall back into my old routine."
- A nurse who asks, "How can we try to change a sick society that crusades to save whales and spotted owls, yet kills babies by the million through abortion?"

Paul challenges us to take up the armor of God and take our place in the battle through spiritual warfare. Prayer is an essential tactic if we want to walk in victory in our own lives and see that the gospel of Christ is made known in the earth.

God provides the Word of God—the Sword of the Spirit—as our primary weapon for confronting the enemy. Jesus wielded this very same weapon to push back the devil's assault in the wilderness temptation. He declared to Satan, "It is written..." and then quoted the Word to him three times (see Luke 4:4-12). Scripture remains our best means of overcoming the evil one.

This book offers an arsenal of verses from both the Old Testament and the New Testament to use in a variety of spiritual battles. Many believers deprive themselves of the help available in the Old Testament, as not so applicable for today's world. But Paul wrote: "All Scripture is God-breathed and is useful for teaching, rebuking, correcting and training in righteousness, so that the man [or woman] of God may be thoroughly equipped for every good work" (2 Timothy 3:16-17).

The Word of God trains and equips us to be effective spiritual warriors. You will also find that praying the Scriptures and declaring God's Word against satanic attacks pushes back the powers of darkness and brings spiritual victory. At the same time, the Holy Spirit will work through the truth of Scripture to correct you, to nourish your spirit, and to strengthen your faith.

This book is not a substitute for your Bible. As you use this prayer guide, may you gain an even greater appreciation for the Word of God. May you increase your knowledge and skill in wielding this Sword of the Spirit, referred to by veteran missionary Arthur Mathews as "the soldier's best friend." "But thanks be to God! He gives us the victory through our Lord Jesus Christ" (1 Corinthians 15:57).

Ruthanne Garlock
Dallas, Texas
April 1992

Prologue

THE APOSTLE PAUL wrote the most complete training manual for spiritual warriors found in Scripture:

> ... be strong in the Lord and in his mighty power. Put on the full armor of God so that you can take your stand against the devil's schemes. For our struggle is not against flesh and blood, but against the rulers, against the authorities, against the powers of this dark world and against the spiritual forces of evil in the heavenly realms. Therefore put on the full armor of God, so that when the day of evil comes, you may be able to stand your ground, and after you have done everything, to stand. Stand firm then, with the belt of truth buckled around your waist, with the breastplate of righteousness in place, and with your feet fitted with the readiness that comes from the gospel of peace. In addition to all this, take up the shield of faith, with which you can extinguish all the flaming arrows of the evil one. Take the helmet of salvation and the sword of the Spirit, which is the word of God. And pray in the Spirit on all occasions with all kinds of prayers and requests. With this in mind, be alert and always keep on praying for all the saints.
>
> **Ephesians 6:10-18**

PART ONE

Preparing for Battle

1

Putting on the Armor

E VEN THOUGH CHRIST'S decisive victory over Satan is complete, we need to acknowledge our own role in enforcing that victory through prayer and spiritual warfare. We face a very real enemy: Satan, meaning "adversary." Since he knows Christ is our only hope of deliverance from his kingdom of darkness, this foe is bent on preventing men, women, and children from embracing the good news of salvation.

If believers are to fulfill Christ's command to take the gospel to every creature, we must not only give of our time and talents, but also commit ourselves to prayer and spiritual warfare on behalf of others.

ARMOR IS CRUCIAL

Only a fool would race into battle without adequate defense. A Christian likewise needs armor to provide protection against "the evil one"—a reference to Satan used in Scripture twenty-four times. Paul teaches believers to put on God's armor "... so that when the day of evil comes, you may be able to stand your ground..." (Ephesians 6:13).

Jesus himself taught his followers a model for prayer which includes this line: "And lead us not into temptation, but deliver us from the evil one" (Matthew 6:13). In his own great priestly prayer for his followers, Jesus asked the Father to "protect them from the evil one" (John 17:15).

Spiritual warfare is far from a struggle between two near-equal powers, God and Satan. We would define it as Satan's efforts involving three basic elements:

1. To destroy the believer's confidence in God and his Son so he or she will forsake the faith.
2. To seduce them through deceptive teaching or their own sin to believe a lie instead of the truth.
3. To prevent unbelievers from hearing a clear presentation of the gospel so they will remain in Satan's kingdom of darkness.

The devil has real power, which Christians would be wise to respect. But as a created being in no way equal with God, his power is limited. Through the cross, Christ disarmed Satan's power and secured victory for the believer who submits to his Lordship (see Colossians 2:15). E.M. Bounds affirms: "To Christ the devil was a very real person. He recognized his personality, felt and acknowledged his power, abhorred his character, and warred against his kingdom.[1]

HOW DOES THE ARMOR WORK?

At the time Paul wrote about the armor of God he was being held under house arrest, a prisoner of Rome guarded by Roman soldiers. Every day he saw them wearing the armor and insignia which identified their status. The Holy Spirit inspired the analogy of the believer as a soldier in God's spiritual army.

Just as a soldier must complete a period of training before being issued battle gear and sent to the front, so must we as Christian soldiers prepare ourselves for spiritual warfare before going to battle. As was the case for a Roman soldier, each piece of our spiritual armor serves a vital function. A single missing part may mean certain defeat when encountering the enemy. May God himself help each of us to be effective in our fight against Satan.

Let's review the six pieces of the full armor presented by Paul in Ephesians 6:10-18. The *belt of truth* was a wide leather or metal belt worn around the lower trunk to keep the armor in place, and to which the sword was attached. The truth of the gospel—salvation by faith in Christ alone—remains the crux of every battle we face. Satan distorts this truth in his attempt to make us doubt God and fall into deception. Jesus most vigorously warned against deception during the last days. (See Matthew 24 and Chapter 24 of this book.)

The forerunner of the bullet-proof vest, the *breastplate of righteousness* protected the soldier's heart and other vital organs. This piece of armor is our only protection against a divided heart. A true soldier must heed Solomon's advice: "Above all else, guard your heart, for it is the wellspring of life" (Proverbs 4:23). If the devil can divide our hearts through footholds like greed, selfishness, and idolatry, then he gains a more secure position by which to defeat us.

The *shoes of peace* symbolize readiness. In oriental cultures, removing one's shoes was an act of reverence, mourning, or submission. When a soldier put on his shoes, it meant he was preparing to report for duty and face the enemy. As Christian soldiers, we wear our shoes of peace to invade enemy territory, bearing the Good News and reconciling humankind to God. "... he has committed to us the message of reconciliation" (2 Corinthians 5:19).

The *shield of faith* refers to the large rectangular shield a soldier used to deflect enemy blows coming from any direction. It was large enough to protect his entire body, as well as protecting all the other pieces of armor. Often a soldier would anoint his shield with oil (a type of the Holy Spirit) in order to reflect the sun's rays and blind the enemy. Rather than "faith in faith," faith in God will strengthen us in battle and enable us to resist the enemy and see him flee (see 1 Peter 5:8-9; James 4:7).

The *helmet of salvation* guards our minds against Satan's flaming arrows (see 1 Thessalonians 5:8). A soldier's helmet not only protected his head in battle but also bore the insignia of his army. Our renewed minds should profoundly influence our behavior, so those in the world recognize that we are Christians in both word and in deed. Keeping our minds renewed in Christ also protects us from deception.

The *sword of the Spirit* is used for both defense and offense. The better we know the Word of God, the more adept we will be at wielding this weapon to oppose the powers of evil. But as Arthur Mathews observes: "Unused weapons do not inflict casualties on the enemy nor win wars.... It is not enough to give mental assent to the fact that a spiritual warfare is going on. Passivity towards our enemy is what the devil wants from us and is his trick to cool the ardor of God's men of war."[2]

VICTORY ASSURED

Everything we need to defeat the enemy has been provided through Christ. Scriptural warnings about "the evil one" and "the day of evil" should be taken seriously. It remains up to us to discipline ourselves, appropriate God's provision, and march into battle. William Gurnall writes:

To put on the armour of God... involves first and foremost a change of heart. The person who boasts that he has confidence in God but does not truly believe with his heart will never be safe in the war zone that separates earth and heaven. If by negligence or choice he fails to put on God's armour and rushes naked into battle, he signs his own death certificate.

... Do not doubt for a moment that Satan will hurl all his fury at those who love God's Word.

... If Satan was too crafty for man in his perfection, how much more dangerous to us now in our maimed condition—for we have never recovered from that first crack Adam's fall gave to our understanding.[3]

Wearing spiritual armor and praying the Word of God is not some sort of "magic formula." Success is not guaranteed if certain words are spoken concerning a specific situation. Prayer and warfare must be solidly based upon faith in God and a relationship with the God whose Word we declare. The Apostle John writes: "Dear friends, if our hearts do not condemn us, we have confidence before God and receive from him anything we ask, because we obey his commands and do what pleases him" (1 John 3:21-22).

SCRIPTURES

The following verses will help spiritual warriors come to a place of faith and readiness so that their prayers can be truly powerful and effective.

... The hour has come for you to wake up from your slumber, because our salvation is nearer now than when we first believed. The night is nearly over; the day is almost here. So let us put aside the deeds of darkness and put on the armor of light.... clothe yourselves with the Lord Jesus Christ, and do not think about how to gratify the desires of the sinful nature. **Romans 13:11-14**

For though we live in the world, we do not wage war as the world does. The weapons we fight with are not the weapons of the world. On the contrary, they have divine power to demolish strongholds. 2 Corinthians 10:3-4

I have posted watchmen on your walls, O Jerusalem;
 they will never be silent day or night.
You who call on the LORD,
 give yourselves no rest,
and give him no rest till he establishes Jerusalem
 and makes her the praise of the earth. Isaiah 62:6-7

Then Moses and the Israelites sang this song to the LORD:
 I will sing to the LORD,
  for he is highly exalted.
 The horse and its rider
  he has hurled into the sea....
 The LORD is a warrior; the LORD is his name. Exodus 15:1-3

Fight the good fight of the faith. Take hold of the eternal life to which you were called when you made your good confession in the presence of many witnesses. 1 Timothy 6:12

Endure hardship with us like a good soldier of Christ Jesus. No one serving as a soldier gets involved in civilian affairs— he wants to please his commanding officer.... I [Paul] endure everything for the sake of the elect, that they too may obtain the salvation that is in Christ Jesus, with eternal glory.
2 Timothy 2:3, 4, 10

Prepare your shields, both large and small, and march out for battle! Jeremiah 46:3

... "Not by might nor by power, but by my Spirit," says the LORD Almighty. Zechariah 4:6

Proclaim this among the nations:
   Prepare for war!
Rouse the warriors!
   Let all the fighting men draw near and attack. Joel 3:9

May the words of my mouth and the meditation of my heart
   be pleasing in your sight,
   O LORD, my Rock and my Redeemer. Psalm 19:14

"Watch and pray so that you will not fall into temptation. The
spirit is willing, but the body is weak." Mark 14:38

Then Jesus told his disciples a parable to show them that they
should always pray and not give up. Luke 18:1

"Why are you sleeping?" he asked them. "Get up and pray so
that you will not fall into temptation." Luke 22:46

Therefore, I urge you, brothers, in view of God's mercy, to
offer your bodies as living sacrifices, holy and pleasing to
God—this is your spiritual act of worship. Romans 12:1

Since we have these promises, dear friends, let us purify ourselves from everything that contaminates body and spirit,
perfecting holiness out of reverence for God. 2 Corinthians 7:1

Have nothing to do with the fruitless deeds of darkness, but
rather expose them.... Be very careful, then, how you live—
not as unwise but as wise, making the most of every opportunity, because the days are evil. Ephesians 5:11, 15-16

Devote yourselves to prayer, being watchful and thankful.
And pray for us, too, that God may open a door for our message, so that we may proclaim the mystery of Christ, for which
I [Paul] am in chains. Pray that I may proclaim it clearly, as I
should. Colossians 4:2-4

For the grace of God that brings salvation has appeared to all men. It teaches us to say "No" to ungodliness and worldly passions, and to live self-controlled, upright and godly lives in this present age.... Titus 2:11-12

Therefore, since we are surrounded by such a great cloud of witnesses, let us throw off everything that hinders and the sin that so easily entangles, and let us run with perseverance the race marked out for us. Let us fix our eyes on Jesus, the author and perfecter of our faith, who for the joy set before him endured the cross, scorning its shame, and sat down at the right hand of the throne of God. Hebrews 12:1-2

Therefore, prepare your minds for action; be self-controlled; set your hope fully on the grace to be given you when Jesus Christ is revealed. As obedient children, do not conform to the evil desires you had when you lived in ignorance. But just as he who called you is holy, so be holy in all you do....

1 Peter 1:13-15

The end of all things is near. Therefore be clear-minded and self-controlled so that you can pray. 1 Peter 4:7

But you, dear friends, build yourselves up in your most holy faith and pray in the Holy Spirit. Jude 1:20

2

Taking Authority in the Name of Jesus

W HAT DID JESUS MEAN WHEN he told his followers, "I have given you authority… to overcome all the power of the enemy…" (Luke 10:19)? He gave to believers the right to exercise power, in his name, over the power of Satan, God's enemy and ours.

One definition of authority is: "the power to rule; the power of one whose will and commands must be obeyed by others."[1] In the beginning, God gave Adam authority to rule or to exercise power in the Garden of Eden (see Genesis 2:15-20). Only one tree was declared off limits. But in yielding to Satan's temptation to eat the fruit of that tree, humankind went beyond the boundary of their God-given authority.

Now sin would have power to rule over the human race. Why was the devil so determined to seduce men and women to sin? As Bible teacher Dean Sherman clarifies:

Satan wanted the authority God had given to man. Although he was on the planet, the devil did not have authority and jurisdiction over the planet.

... Satan knew that man could use or misuse the authority given to him. When man disobeyed God, Satan was able to usurp man's authority. Just as God transferred some of his authority to man, so man passed it on to Satan... but Satan can only use it through man. He can only *influence* the world to the degree that man chooses to sin and live in disobedience to God. This is what we might call the balance of power.[2]

RELATIONSHIP WITH JESUS

Through his sacrificial death, burial, and resurrection, Christ defeated Satan's power and received from God authority over all angels and powers (see 1 Peter 3:18-22). Now humankind, through Christ, can regain the authority he had squandered. Dean Sherman explains further:

... The balance of power on the earth rests with man in the name of Jesus Christ. The authority is complete in man as long as man is in relationship with God through Jesus Christ. With our authority comes the reponsibility to use it for God's purposes. If we don't rebuke the devil, he will not be rebuked. If we don't drive him back, he will not leave. It is up to us. Satan knows of our authority, but hopes we will stay ignorant. We must be as convinced of our authority as the devil is.[3]

Relationship is the key. Without a close relationship with Christ, we have no basis for taking authority over Satan and he knows it. But God has placed Christ at his own right hand in heaven in a position of authority over all other powers. And because we're a part of his body, the Church, we can use his name with authority. Scripture declares:

... [God's] power is like the working of his mighty strength, which he exerted in Christ when he raised him from the dead and seated him at his right hand in the heavenly realms, far above all rule and authority, power and dominion, and every title that can be given, not only in the present age but also in the one to come. And God placed all things under his feet and appointed him to be head over everything for the church, which is his body....

Ephesians 1:19-23

The Book of Acts records the story of a group of men who tried—to their own sorrow—to cast out demons in the name of Jesus when they had no relationship with him. The account reads:

Some Jews who went around driving out evil spirits tried to invoke the name of the Lord Jesus over those who were demon-possessed. They would say, "In the name of Jesus, whom Paul preaches, I command you to come out."... [One day] the evil spirit answered them, "Jesus I know, and I know about Paul, but who are you?" Then the man who had the evil spirit jumped on them and overpowered them all. He gave them such a beating that they ran out of the house naked and bleeding. **Acts 19:13, 15-16**

JESUS SPOKE WITH AUTHORITY

... the crowds were amazed at his teaching, because he taught as one who had authority, and not as their teachers of the law.

Matthew 7:28-29

"... so that you may know that the Son of Man has authority on earth to forgive sins...." Then he said to the paralytic, "Get up, take your mat and go home." And the man got up and went home. When the crowd saw this, they were filled with awe; and they praised God, who had given such authority to men. **Matthew 9:6-8**

Seeing a fig tree by the road, he went up to it but found nothing on it except leaves. Then he said to it, "May you never bear fruit again!" Immediately the tree withered.

When the disciples saw this, they were amazed. "How did the fig tree wither so quickly?" they asked.

Jesus replied, "I tell you the truth, if you have faith and do not doubt, not only can you do what was done to the fig tree, but also you can say to this mountain, 'Go, throw yourself into the sea,' and it will be done. If you believe, you will receive whatever you ask for in prayer." Matthew 21:19-22

The people were amazed at his teaching, because he taught them as one who had authority, not as the teachers of the law.... The people were all so amazed that they asked each other, "What is this? A new teaching—and with authority! He even gives orders to evil spirits and they obey him." Mark 1:22, 27

"... I lay down my life for the sheep.... No one takes it from me, but I lay it down of my own accord. I have authority to lay it down and authority to take it up again. This command I received from my Father." John 10:15, 18

GOD GAVE AUTHORITY TO CHRIST

Therefore God exalted him [Christ] to the highest place
   and gave him the name that is above every name,
that at the name of Jesus every knee should bow,
   in heaven and on earth and under the earth,
and every tongue confess that Jesus Christ is Lord,
   to the glory of God the Father. Philippians 2:9-11

[Christ] is the image of the invisible God, the firstborn over all creation. For by him all things were created: things in heaven and on earth, visible and invisible, whether thrones or powers or rulers or authorities; all things were created by him and for him. He is before all things, and in him all things hold together. And he is the head of the body, the church; he is the beginning and the firstborn from among the dead, so that in everything he might have the supremacy. For God was pleased to have all his fullness dwell in him, and through him to reconcile to himself all things, whether things on earth or things in heaven.... **Colossians 1:15-20**

In my vision at night I looked, and there before me was one like a son of man, coming with the clouds of heaven. He approached the Ancient of Days and was led into his presence. He was given authority, glory and sovereign power; all peoples, nations and men of every language worshiped him. His dominion is an everlasting dominion that will not pass away, and his kingdom is one that will never be destroyed.

Daniel 7:13-14

PRAYING FOR THE UNPRECEDENTED

Few believers pray and exercise faith at the level Christ intended for his followers. J. Oswald Sanders challenges us to move up to the level of "audacious praying." He writes:

Seldom do our petitions rise above the level of natural thought or previous experience. Do we ever dare to pray for the unprecedented? The whole atmosphere of the age tends to make us minimize what we can expect of God, and yet His Word reveals that the extent of legitimate expectation is literally without limits.

As though to anticipate our reluctance to ask audaciously, God employs every universal term in our language in his promises to the praying soul. Here they are: Whatsoever, wheresoever, whensoever, whosoever, all, any, every. ... Trace [these] words in their relation to prayer and note how they encourage large petitions.[4]

CHRIST'S AUTHORITY GIVEN TO BELIEVERS

When Jesus had called the Twelve together, he gave them power and authority to drive out all demons and to cure diseases, and he sent them out to preach the kingdom of God and to heal the sick. Luke 9:1-2

"I have given you authority to trample on snakes and scorpions and to overcome all the power of the enemy; nothing will harm you." Luke 10:19

The LORD will make you the head, not the tail. If you pay attention to the commands of the LORD your God that I give you this day and carefully follow them, you will always be at the top, never at the bottom. Deuteronomy 28:13

"I will give you the keys of the kingdom of heaven; whatever you bind on earth will be bound in heaven, and whatever you loose on earth will be loosed in heaven." Matthew 16:19

Then Jesus came to them and said, "All authority in heaven and on earth has been given to me. Therefore go and make disciples of all nations, baptizing them in the name of the Father and of the Son and of the Holy Spirit, and teaching them to obey everything I have commanded you. And surely I am with you always, to the very end of the age." Matthew 28:18-20

Calling the Twelve to him, he sent them out two by two and gave them authority over evil spirits.... They drove out many demons and anointed many sick people with oil and healed them. Mark 6:7, 13

[Jesus] said to them, "... And these signs will accompany those who believe: in my name they will drive out demons; they will speak in new tongues; they will pick up snakes with their hands; and when they drink deadly poison, it will not hurt them at all; they will place their hands on sick people, and they will get well." **Mark 16:15-18**

"You did not choose me, but I chose you and appointed you to go and bear fruit—fruit that will last. Then the Father will give you whatever you ask in my name." **John 15:16**

... Jesus said, "Peace be with you! As the Father has sent me, I am sending you." And with that he breathed on them and said, "Receive the Holy Spirit...." **John 20:21-22**

... Repent and be baptized, every one of you, in the name of Jesus Christ for the forgiveness of your sins. And you will receive the gift of the Holy Spirit.... **Acts 2:38**

This girl followed Paul and the rest of us, shouting, "These men are servants of the Most High God, who are telling you the way to be saved." She kept this up for many days. Finally Paul became so troubled that he turned around and said to the spirit, "In the name of Jesus Christ I command you to come out of her!" At that moment the spirit left her.

Acts 16:17-18

Through him and for his name's sake, we received grace and apostleship to call people from among all the Gentiles to the obedience that comes from faith. And you also are among those who are called to belong to Jesus Christ. **Romans 1:5-6**

Unlike so many, we do not peddle the word of God for profit. On the contrary, in Christ we speak before God with sincerity, like men sent from God. **2 Corinthians 2:17**

Finally, be strong in the Lord and in his mighty power. Put on the full armor of God so that you can take your stand against the devil's schemes.... In addition to all this, take up the shield of faith, with which you can extinguish all the flaming arrows of the evil one. **Ephesians 6:10-11, 16**

... you have been given fullness in Christ, who is the head over every power and authority....

... whatever you do, whether in word or deed, do it all in the name of the Lord Jesus, giving thanks to God the Father through him. Colossians 2:10; 3:17

These, then, are the things you should teach. Encourage and rebuke with all authority. Do not let anyone despise you.

Titus 2:15

Submit yourselves, then, to God. Resist the devil, and he will flee from you. James 4:7

To him who overcomes and does my will to the end, I will give authority over the nations... just as I have received authority from my Father. Revelation 2:26-27

3

The Power of the Blood of Jesus

T HE BLOOD OF JESUS, the means of our redemption, is the most precious physical substance ever to touch the earth. In obedience to the law, the Jewish people had for generations offered animal sacrifices to atone for their sins and to satisfy the justice of God.

But when Jesus came to earth, he fulfilled the law by becoming the perfect sacrifice, atoning for the sin of all humankind. Abolishing the need for animal sacrifice, his blood is not only precious but powerful. Why did Jesus submit to a bloody death on a cross, when all the power of the universe was and is available to him? The great expositor G. Campbell Morgan explains:

> ... He was not only the Sin-bearer; in the activities of that dark hour, he was the Sin-destroyer; in some infinite transaction beyond human power of thought, he destroyed the works of the devil.

... In order to establish the Kingdom he must himself gather the sin to himself, and deal with it, grapple with it, master it, negate it; and, emerging from the struggle victorious, communicate life, in the power of which other souls shall be able to enter into the same struggle, and with a like result.[1]

When we confess our sins and repent of our rebellion against God, we receive forgiveness and cleansing through the blood of Jesus. His blood opens the door to reconciliation with the Father. It delivers us from the curse and power of sin, along with the fear of death. It is also the basis of our authority over the enemy. H.A. Maxwell Whyte writes:

We can hardly claim to be under the Blood of Jesus if we are walking in deliberate disobedience.... Sprinkling of the Blood of Jesus without obedience to the Word of God will avail us nothing.

... In the natural world, we would have no difficulty understanding how to apply disinfectant to an infection. We would take the disinfectant and sprinkle or pour it upon the infection, and the result would be that all germs and living organisms present in that infection would die. Now we should have no difficulty in doing the same thing spiritually. Wherever Satan is at work, we must apply the only corrective antidote there is—the Blood of Jesus. There is absolutely no alternative, no substitute. Prayer, praise, worship and devotion all have their part in our approach to God; but the Blood of Jesus is the only effective counter-agent to corruption.[2]

To "apply the blood of Jesus" over ourselves and our loved ones in prayer and spiritual warfare is a way of declaring to the devil that his blood creates a boundary he cannot violate. Only believers who have by faith appropriated Christ's sacrifice for their sins can apply this precious blood. But we must not treat this as some "magic formula" that guarantees protection from adversity.

In fact, Jesus told his followers: "No servant is greater than his master. If they persecuted me, they will persecute you also...." (John 15:20). And Paul wrote, "... everyone who wants to live a godly life in Christ Jesus will be persecuted..." (2 Timothy 3:12).

Being under the blood of Jesus does mean that any attempt of the enemy to destroy us will ultimately end in his own defeat, just as Jesus' death on the cross sealed his doom. As we read in Scripture: "None of the rulers of this age understood it [God's wisdom], for if they had, they would not have crucified the Lord of glory (1 Corinthians 2:8).

The practice of applying the blood is based upon the account in Exodus 12. God instructed the people of Israel to kill a sacrificial lamb and place the blood upon their doorframes, thereby protecting their households from the plague of death he would send upon the Egyptians. That lamb was a foreshadowing of the Lamb of God, Jesus himself, whose sacrifice at Calvary would deliver all humankind from spiritual death.

SCRIPTURES

Arthur Mathews wrote, "... Blessed is that intercessor who knows how to use the power of the blood in spiritual warfare." [3]

You can do that by declaring aloud the power of Jesus' blood by reciting these Scriptures:

The blood will be a sign for you on the houses where you are; and when I see the blood, I will pass over you. No destructive plague will touch you when I strike Egypt.

... When the LORD goes through the land to strike down

the Egyptians, he will see the blood on the top and sides of the doorframe and will pass over that doorway, and he will not permit the destroyer to enter your houses and strike you down. **Exodus 12:13, 23**

For the life of a creature is in the blood, and I have given it to you to make atonement for yourselves on the altar; it is the blood that makes atonement for one's life. **Leviticus 17:11**

But only the high priest entered the inner room, and that only once a year, and never without blood, which he offered for himself and for the sins the people had committed in ignorance....

He [Christ] did not enter by means of the blood of goats and calves; but he entered the Most Holy Place once for all by his own blood, having obtained eternal redemption....

How much more, then, will the blood of Christ, who through the eternal Spirit offered himself unblemished to God, cleanse our consciences from acts that lead to death, so that we may serve the living God! **Hebrews 9:7, 12, 14**

Then he took the cup, gave thanks and offered it to them, saying, "Drink from it, all of you. This is my blood of the covenant, which is poured out for many for the forgiveness of sins." **Matthew 26:27-28**

When Judas, who had betrayed him, saw that Jesus was condemned, he was seized with remorse and returned the thirty silver coins to the chief priests and the elders. "I have sinned," he said, "for I have betrayed innocent blood." **Matthew 27:3-4**

Therefore, whoever eats the bread or drinks the cup of the Lord in an unworthy manner will be guilty of sinning against the body and blood of the Lord. A man ought to examine himself before he eats of the bread and drinks of the cup.

1 Corinthians 11:27-28

Keep watch over yourselves and all the flock of which the Holy Spirit has made you overseers. Be shepherds of the church of God, which he bought with his own blood. Acts 20:28

God presented him as a sacrifice of atonement, through faith in his blood. He did this to demonstrate his justice, because in his forbearance he had left the sins committed beforehand unpunished—he did it to demonstrate his justice... so as to be just and the one who justifies those who have faith in Jesus.
Romans 3:25-26

Since we have now been justified by his blood, how much more shall we be saved from God's wrath through him! For if, when we were God's enemies, we were reconciled to him through the death of his Son, how much more, having been reconciled, shall we be saved through his life! Romans 5:9-10

... In love he predestined us to be adopted as his sons through Jesus Christ.... In him we have redemption through his blood, the forgiveness of sins, in accordance with the riches of God's grace that he lavished on us with all wisdom and understanding. Ephesians 1:4-5, 7-8

... at that time you were separate from Christ, excluded from citizenship in Israel and foreigners to the covenants of the promise, without hope and without God in the world. But now in Christ Jesus you who once were far away have been brought near through the blood of Christ. Ephesians 2:12-13

For God was pleased to have all his fullness dwell in him [Christ], and through him to reconcile to himself all things... by making peace through his blood, shed on the cross.
Colossians 1:19, 20

Since the children have flesh and blood, he too shared in their humanity so that by his death he might destroy him who holds the power of death—that is, the devil—and free those who all their lives were held in slavery by their fear of death.... He had to be made like his brothers in every way... that he might make atonement for the sins of the people.

Hebrews 2:14-15, 17

... the law requires that nearly everything be cleansed with blood, and without the shedding of blood there is no forgiveness.

... but now he [Christ] has appeared once for all at the end of the ages to do away with sin by the sacrifice of himself.

Hebrews 9:22, 26

... since we have confidence to enter the Most Holy Place by the blood of Jesus, by a new and living way opened for us through the curtain, that is, his body... let us draw near to God with a sincere heart in full assurance of faith.... Let us hold unswervingly to the hope we profess, for he who promised is faithful. **Hebrews 10:19-20, 22-23**

May the God of peace, who through the blood of the eternal covenant brought back from the dead our Lord Jesus... equip you with everything good for doing his will.... **Hebrews 13:20-21**

For you know that it was not with perishable things such as silver or gold that you were redeemed from the empty way of life handed down to you from your forefathers, but with the precious blood of Christ, a lamb without blemish or defect. He was chosen before the creation of the world, but was revealed in these last times for your sake. **1 Peter 1:18-20**

... if we walk in the light, as he is in the light, we have fellowship with one another, and the blood of Jesus, his Son, purifies us from all sin. **1 John 1:7**

This is the one who came by water and blood—Jesus Christ. He did not come by water only, but by water and blood. And it is the Spirit who testifies, because the Spirit is the truth. For there are three that testify: the Spirit, the water and the blood; and the three are in agreement. 1 John 5:6-8

... to him [Jesus Christ] who loves us and has freed us from our sins by his blood, and has made us to be a kingdom and priests to serve his God and Father—to him be glory and power for ever and ever! Amen. Revelation 1:5-6

... the four living creatures and the twenty-four elders fell down before the Lamb. Each one had a harp and they were holding golden bowls full of incense, which are the prayers of the saints. And they sang a new song:

"You are worthy to take the scroll
and to open its seals,
because you were slain,
and with your blood you purchased men for God
from every tribe and language and people and nation.
You have made them to be a kingdom and priests to serve
our God,
and they will reign on the earth." Revelation 5:8-10

... "These are they who have come out of the great tribulation; they have washed their robes and made them white in the blood of the Lamb." Revelation 7:14

They overcame him [Satan]
by the blood of the Lamb
and by the word of their testimony;
they did not love their lives so much
as to shrink from death. Revelation 12:11

I saw heaven standing open and there before me was a white horse, whose rider is called Faithful and True. With justice he judges and makes war. His eyes are like blazing fire, and on his head are many crowns. He has a name written on him that no one knows but he himself. He is dressed in a robe dipped in blood, and his name is the Word of God. The armies of heaven were following him, riding on white horses and dressed in fine linen, white and clean. Out of his mouth comes a sharp sword with which to strike down the nations. "He will rule them with an iron scepter." He treads the winepress of the fury of the wrath of God Almighty. On his robe and on his thigh he has this name written: KING OF KINGS AND LORD OF LORDS. **Revelation 19:11-16**

4

The Power of the Word of God

THE ONLY PIECE OF THE spiritual warrior's armor which is both offensive and defensive is named last on Paul's list: "the sword of the Spirit, which is the word of God" (Ephesians 6:17). William Gurnall aptly describes this piece of armor:

> The sword is the weapon continually used by soldiers to defend themselves and to rout their enemies. Thus it illustrates the most excellent use of God's Word, by which the believer both defends himself and cuts down his enemies.
>
> ... Because Satan is a spirit we must fight him with spiritual arms. And the Word is a spiritual sword.
>
> ... God's army overcomes every enemy by one of two ways—conversion or destruction. The Word of God is the sword which effects both—it has two edges.[1]

This two-edged sword is the very weapon Jesus used to withstand Satan in the wilderness. Scripture makes it clear that Jesus had studied Scripture and filled his mind with its truth.

that Jesus had studied Scripture and filled his mind with its truth. In the moment of crisis, his sword was sharp and ready. All it took to defeat the enemy was "every word that comes from the mouth of the Lord" (Deuteronomy 8:3).

This passage speaks of the power of the Word: "For the word of God is living and active. Sharper than any double-edged sword, it penetrates even to dividing soul and spirit, joints and marrow; it judges the thoughts and attitudes of the heart" (Hebrews 4:12).

Bible teacher Roy Hicks, Sr., offers this explanation:

> The term for "word" here [in Hebrews 4:12] is the Greek word *logos*, which commonly indicates the expression of a complete idea and is used in referring to the Holy Scriptures. It contrasts with *rhema*, which generally refers to a word spoken or given. This recommends our understanding the difference between *all* the Bible and the *single* promise or promises the Holy Spirit may bring to our mind from the Word of God. When facing a situation of need, trial, or difficulty, the promises of God may become a *rhema* to you; that is, a weapon of the Spirit, "the word of God" [Ephesians 6:17]. Its authority is that this "word" comes from the Bible—God's Word—the completed *logos*.[3]

SCRIPTURES

I [God] make known the end from the beginning,
  from ancient times, what is still to come.
I say: My purpose will stand,
  and I will do all that I please....
What I have said, that will I bring about;
  what I have planned, that will I do. Isaiah 46:10-11

... so is my word that goes out from my mouth:
It will not return to me empty,
  but will accomplish what I desire
and achieve the purpose for which I sent it. Isaiah 55:11

"As for me, this is my covenant with them," says the LORD. "My Spirit, who is on you, and my words that I have put in your mouth will not depart from your mouth, or from the mouths of your children, or from the mouths of their descendants from this time on and forever," says the LORD.   Isaiah 59:21

Then the LORD said to Moses, "Write down these words, for in accordance with these words I have made a covenant with you and with Israel."   Exodus 34:27

If anyone does not listen to my words that the prophet speaks in my name, I myself will call him to account.   Deuteronomy 18:19

... "Take to heart all the words I have solemnly declared to you this day, so that you may command your children to obey carefully all the words of this law. They are not just idle words for you—they are your life...."   Deuteronomy 32:46-47

When the king heard the words of the Book of the Law, he tore his robes.... "Go and inquire of the LORD for me and for the people and for all Judah about what is written in this book that has been found. Great is the LORD's anger that burns against us because our fathers have not obeyed the words of this book...."   2 Kings 22:11, 13

... they mocked God's messengers, despised his words and scoffed at his prophets until the wrath of the LORD was aroused against his people and there was no remedy.

2 Chronicles 36:16

My soul faints with longing for your salvation,
    but I have put my hope in your word....
Your word is a lamp to my feet
    and a light for my path....
Your statutes are my heritage forever;
    they are the joy of my heart.
My heart is set on keeping your decrees
    to the very end. Psalm 119:81, 105, 111-112

The unfolding of your words gives light;
　　it gives understanding to the simple....
All your words are true;
　　all your righteous laws are eternal.　Psalm 119:130, 160

I will bow down toward your holy temple
　　and will praise your name
　　for your love and your faithfulness,
for you have exalted above all things
　　your name and your word.　Psalm 138:2

Let them praise the name of the LORD,
　　for he commanded and they were created.
He set them in place for ever and ever;
　　he gave a decree that will never pass away.　Psalm 148:5-6

Every word of God is flawless;
　　he is a shield to those who take refuge in him.　Proverbs 30:5

The LORD said to me, "You have seen correctly, for I am watching to see that my word is fulfilled."　Jeremiah 1:12

"... I will make my words in your mouth a fire..."　Jeremiah 5:14

When your words came, I ate them;
　　they were my joy and my heart's delight,
for I bear your name,
　　O LORD God Almighty.　Jeremiah 15:16

"Is not my word like fire," declares the LORD, "and like a hammer that breaks a rock in pieces?"　Jeremiah 23:29

The Lord has done what he planned;
　　he has fulfilled his word,
　　which he decreed long ago....
Who can speak and have it happen
　　if the Lord has not decreed it?　Lamentations 2:17; 3:37

You must speak my words to them, whether they listen or fail to listen, for they are rebellious....

"... None of my words will be delayed any longer; whatever I say will be fulfilled, declares the Sovereign LORD."

Ezekiel 2:7; 12:28

"... by your words you will be acquitted, and by your words you will be condemned." **Matthew 12:37**

"Heaven and earth will pass away, but my words will never pass away." **Matthew 24:35**

For with God nothing is ever impossible, and no word from God shall be without power or impossible of fulfillment.

Luke 1:37, AMP

In the beginning was the Word, and the Word was with God, and the Word was God.... In him was life, and that life was the light of men. **John 1:1, 4**

For the one whom God has sent speaks the words of God, for God gives the Spirit without limit.... And because of his words many more became believers. **John 3:34; 4:41**

"I tell you the truth, whoever hears my word and believes him who sent me has eternal life and will not be condemned; he has crossed over from death to life....

"... if anyone keeps my word, he will never see death."

John 5:24; 8:51

"The Spirit gives life; the flesh counts for nothing. The words I have spoken to you are spirit and they are life."

... Simon Peter answered him, "Lord, to whom shall we go? You have the words of eternal life...." **John 6:63, 68**

"If you remain in me and my words remain in you, ask whatever you wish, and it will be given you." **John 15:7**

... faith comes from hearing the message, and the message is heard through the word of Christ. **Romans 10:17**

... because our gospel came to you not simply with words, but also with power, with the Holy Spirit and with deep conviction.... 1 Thessalonians 1:5

... God's word is not chained. 2 Timothy 2:9

For you have been born again, not of perishable seed, but of imperishable, through the living and enduring word of God. For,
   "... the grass withers and the flowers fall,
      but the word of the Lord stands forever."
   And this is the word that was preached to you. 1 Peter 1:23-25

... With the Lord a day is like a thousand years, and a thousand years are like a day. The Lord is not slow in keeping his promise, as some understand slowness. He is patient with you, not wanting anyone to perish, but everyone to come to repentance. 2 Peter 3:8-9

... the word of God lives in you, and you have overcome the evil one. 1 John 2:14

... among the lampstands was someone "like a son of man," dressed in a robe reaching down to his feet and with a golden sash around his chest. His head and hair were white like wool, as white as snow, and his eyes were like blazing fire... and out of his mouth came a sharp double-edged sword. His face was like the sun shining in all its brilliance. Revelation 1:13-14, 16

... these are the words of him who has the sharp, double-edged sword.... Repent therefore! Otherwise, I will soon come to you and will fight against them with the sword of my mouth.... Revelation 2:12, 16

He who was seated on the throne said, "I am making everything new!" Then he said, "Write this down, for these words are trustworthy and true." Revelation 21:5

5

The Weapon
of Praise

Praise. adulation. commendation. We heap such sentiments on people after achieving a goal or performing in some way. But keen spiritual warriors learn the power of praising God *before* seeing evidence of his intervention in the prayer concern. We can offer thanksgiving with such confidence because of who he is—a God of love, faithfulness, holiness, and justice.

Scripture declares, "He is the Rock, his works are perfect, and all his ways are just. A faithful God who does no wrong, upright and just is he" (Deuteronomy 32:4). When we praise God despite negative circumstances, we affirm his power and victory over those circumstances.

A.W. Tozer wrote, "True Christian joy is the heart's harmonious response to the Lord's song of love."[1] That harmonious response bursts forth in praise. Three important results flow from our praise:

1. God receives glory.
2. Our faith is increased and we are energized by the joy of the Lord that accompanies praise.
3. The enemy is terrified and his plans confounded.

Since the devil knows the power of praise, he works diligently to discourage Christians from using this potent weapon against his dark kingdom. Jack Taylor writes:

> Nothing terrifies the devil and his demons like praise. Praise brings the consciousness of the presence of God with all that accompanies it. The liars from the pit cannot effectively market their wares in an atmosphere of praise. Since it is a garment, we can make a choice to put it on as we do a shirt, a blouse, or a coat. The constant wearing of it will ward off the spirits of depression, discouragement, and despair.
>
> ... Praise, the continuing exercise of heaven, is clearly etched into the memory of the devil and every other fallen angel. The memory of the aborted revolution, in which they all lost their lofty positions, is haunting and all too clear in their minds.... When they hear biblical praises they are driven to panic. They are irritated and devastated.... Their ranks are broken. Like metal scratching glass is the sound of praises to them.[2]

Paul and Silas, beaten and thrown into prison for casting a demon out of a slave girl, found praise most effective even in the midst of seemingly impossible situations (see Acts 16:16-36). They praised God in spite of the circumstances, knowing they could trust him completely, no matter what the outcome. The enemy simply cannot overcome that kind of faith, and his plans are plunged into confusion. Declare the following verses of praise from Scripture to set the enemy into confusion and to push back the forces of darkness and despair. Some of these passages can also be sung, which can multiply the effectiveness of praise.

SCRIPTURES

Rejoice in the Lord always. I will say it again: Rejoice!

Philippians 4:4

Through Jesus, therefore, let us continually offer to God a sacrifice of praise—the fruit of lips that confess his name.

Hebrews 13:15

... I will sing to the LORD,
    for he is highly exalted.
The horse and its rider
    he has hurled into the sea.
The LORD is my strength and my song;
    he has become my salvation.
He is my God, and I will praise him,
    my father's God, and I will exalt him.   **Exodus 15:1-2**

He is your praise; he is your God, who performed for you those great and awesome wonders you saw with your own eyes.   **Deuteronomy 10:21**

I will proclaim the name of the LORD.
    Oh, praise the greatness of our God!
He is the Rock, his works are perfect,
    and all his ways are just.
A faithful God who does no wrong,
    upright and just is he....
Rejoice, O nations, with his people,
    for he will avenge the blood of his servants;
he will take vengeance on his enemies
    and make atonement for his land and people.

Deuteronomy 32:3-4, 43

My heart rejoices in the LORD;
    in the LORD my horn is lifted high.
My mouth boasts over my enemies,
    for I delight in your deliverance.
There is no one holy like the LORD;

there is no one besides you;
there is no Rock like our God. 1 Samuel 2:1-2

I call to the Lord, who is worthy of praise,
and I am saved from my enemies....
I will praise you, O LORD, among the nations;
I will sing praises to your name. 2 Samuel 22:4, 50

Sing to him, sing praise to him;
tell of all his wonderful acts....
For great is the LORD and most worthy of praise;
he is to be feared above all gods....
Let the heavens rejoice, let the earth be glad;
let them say among the nations, "The LORD reigns!"
1 Chronicles 16:9, 25, 31

David said, " ... four thousand are to praise the LORD with the
musical instruments I have provided for that purpose."
... They were also to stand every morning to thank and
praise the LORD. They were to do the same in the evening....
They were to serve before the LORD regularly in the proper
number and in the way prescribed for them.
1 Chronicles 23:4-5, 30-31

... praise be to you, O LORD,
God of our father Israel,
from everlasting to everlasting.
Yours, O LORD, is the greatness and the power
and the glory and the majesty and the splendor,
for everything in heaven and earth is yours.
Yours, O LORD, is the kingdom;
you are exalted as head over all.
Wealth and honor come from you;
you are the ruler of all things.
In your hands are strength and power
to exalt and give strength to all. 1 Chronicles 29:10-12

All the Levites who were musicians... stood on the east side of the altar, dressed in fine linen and playing cymbals, harps and lyres. They were accompanied by 120 priests sounding trumpets. The trumpeters and singers joined in unison, as with one voice, to give praise and thanks to the LORD. Accompanied by trumpets, cymbals and other instruments, they raised their voices in praise to the LORD and sang:

"He is good;
    his love endures forever."

Then the temple of the LORD was filled with a cloud, and the priests could not perform their service because of the cloud, for the glory of the LORD filled the temple of God.

2 Chronicles 5:12-14

... Jehoshaphat appointed men to sing to the LORD and to praise him for the splendor of his holiness as they went out at the head of the army, saying:

"Give thanks to the LORD,
    for his love endures forever."

As they began to sing and praise, the LORD set ambushes against the men... who were invading Judah, and they were defeated.... Then, led by Jehoshaphat, all the men of Judah and Jerusalem returned joyfully to Jerusalem, for the LORD had given them cause to rejoice over their enemies.

2 Chronicles 20:21-22, 27

O LORD, our Lord,
    how majestic is your name in all the earth!
You have set your glory
    above the heavens.
From the lips of children and infants
    you have ordained praise
because of your enemies,
    to silence the foe and the avenger. **Psalm 8:1-2**

I will praise you, O LORD, with all my heart;
    I will tell of all your wonders.

I will be glad and rejoice in you;
    I will sing praise to your name, O Most High.
My enemies turn back;
    they stumble and perish before you. **Psalm 9:1-3**

Praise be to the LORD,
    for he showed his wonderful love to me
    when I was in a besieged city....
In God we make our boast all day long,
    and we will praise your name forever. **Psalms 31:21; 44:8**

But may all who seek you
    rejoice and be glad in you;
may those who love your salvation always say,
    "The LORD be exalted!" **Psalm 40:16**

Clap your hands, all you nations;
    shout to God with cries of joy.
How awesome is the LORD Most High,
    the great King over all the earth!
He subdued nations under us,
    peoples under our feet. **Psalm 47:1-3**

But may the righteous be glad
    and rejoice before God;
    may they be happy and joyful.
Sing to God, sing praise to his name,
    extol him who rides on the clouds—
his name is the LORD—
    and rejoice before him. **Psalm 68:3-4**

Praise be to the LORD God, the God of Israel,
    who alone does marvelous deeds.
Praise be to his glorious name forever;
    may the whole earth be filled with his glory.
Amen and Amen. **Psalm 72:18-19**

I will praise you, O Lord my God, with all my heart;
    I will glorify your name forever.

For great is your love toward me;
    you have delivered me from the depths of the grave.
Psalm 86:12-13

Sing to the LORD a new song;
    sing to the LORD, all the earth.
Sing to the LORD, praise his name;
    proclaim his salvation day after day.
Declare his glory among the nations,
    his marvelous deeds among all peoples.
For great is the LORD and most worthy of praise;
    he is to be feared above all gods. **Psalm 96:1-4**

I will sing to the LORD all my life;
    I will sing praise to my God as long as I live. **Psalm 104:33**

I will praise you, O LORD, among the nations;
    I will sing of you among the peoples. **Psalm 108:3**

Praise the LORD, all you nations;
    extol him, all you peoples.
For great is his love toward us,
    and the faithfulness of the LORD endures forever.
Praise the LORD. **Psalm 117:1-2**

Accept, O LORD, the willing praise of my mouth,
    and teach me your laws....
Let me live that I may praise you,
    and may your laws sustain me. **Psalm 119:108, 175**

I will praise you, O LORD, with all my heart;
    before the "gods" I will sing your praise.
I will bow down toward your holy temple
    and will praise your name
    for your love and your faithfulness,
for you have exalted above all things
    your name and your word....
May all the kings of the earth praise you, O LORD,
    when they hear the words of your mouth. **Psalm 138:1-4**

Set me free from my prison,
    that I may praise your name.
Then the righteous will gather about me
    because of your goodness to me.   **Psalm 142:7**

Praise the LORD.
Sing to the LORD a new song,
    his praise in the assembly of the saints....
Let them praise his name with dancing
    and make music to him with tambourine and harp....
May the praise of God be in their mouths
    and a double-edged sword in their hands,
to inflict vengeance on the nations
    and punishment on the peoples,
to bind their kings with fetters,
    their nobles with shackles of iron,
to carry out the sentence written against them....
                                    Psalm 149:1, 3, 6-9

Praise the LORD.
Praise God in his sanctuary;
    praise him in his mighty heavens.
Praise him for his acts of power;
    praise him for his surpassing greatness.
Praise him with the sounding of the trumpet,
    praise him with the harp and lyre,
praise him with tambourine and dancing,
    praise him with the strings and flute,
praise him with the clash of cymbals,
    praise him with resounding cymbals.
Let everything that has breath praise the LORD.
Praise the LORD.   **Psalm 150:1-6**

O LORD, you are my God;
I will exalt you and praise your name,
    for in perfect faithfulness
you have done marvelous things,

things planned long ago....
In that day they will say,
"Surely this is our God;
    we trusted in him, and he saved us.
This is the LORD, we trusted in him;
    let us rejoice and be glad in his salvation." **Isaiah 25:1, 9**

For the grave cannot praise you,
    death cannot sing your praise;
those who go down to the pit
    cannot hope for your faithfulness.
The living, the living—they praise you,
    as I am doing today;
fathers tell their children
    about your faithfulness. **Isaiah 38:18-19**

No longer will violence be heard in your land,
    nor ruin or destruction within your borders,
but you will call your walls Salvation
 and your gates Praise. **Isaiah 60:18**

... "Praise be to the name of God for ever and ever;
    wisdom and power are his.
He changes times and seasons;
    he sets up kings and deposes them.
He gives wisdom to the wise
    and knowledge to the discerning.
He reveals deep and hidden things;
    he knows what lies in darkness,
    and light dwells with him.
I thank and praise you, O God of my fathers:
    You have given me wisdom and power...." **Daniel 2:20-23**

Sing to the LORD!
    Give praise to the LORD!
He rescues the life of the needy
    from the hands of the wicked. **Jeremiah 20:13**

Though the fig tree does not bud
   and there are no grapes on the vines,
though the olive crop fails
   and the fields produce no food,
though there are no sheep in the pen
   and no cattle in the stalls,
yet I will rejoice in the LORD,
   I will be joyful in God my Savior.
The Sovereign LORD is my strength;
   he makes my feet like the feet of a deer.... **Habakkuk 3:17-19**

Rejoice greatly, O Daughter of Zion!
   Shout, Daughter of Jerusalem!
See, your king comes to you,
   righteous and having salvation,
gentle and riding on a donkey,
   on a colt, the foal of a donkey. **Zechariah 9:9**

And Mary said:
   "My soul glorifies the Lord
      and my spirit rejoices in God my Savior...." **Luke 1:46-47**

At that time Jesus, full of joy through the Holy Spirit, said, "I praise you, Father, Lord of heaven and earth, because you have hidden these things from the wise and learned, and revealed them to little children...." **Luke 10:21**

"... a time is coming and has now come when the true worshipers will worship the Father in spirit and truth, for they are the kind of worshipers the Father seeks. God is spirit, and his worshipers must worship in spirit and in truth." **John 4:23-24**

Praise be to the God and Father of our Lord Jesus Christ, who has blessed us in the heavenly realms with every spiritual blessing in Christ. **Ephesians 1:3**

... to the only God our Savior be glory, majesty, power and authority, through Jesus Christ our Lord, before all ages, now and forevermore! Amen. **Jude 1:25**

... the twenty-four elders fall down before him who sits on the throne, and worship him who lives for ever and ever. They lay their crowns before the throne and say:

"You are worthy, our Lord and God,
to receive glory and honor and power,
for you created all things,
and by your will they were created
and have their being." **Revelation 4:10-11**

Then one of the elders said to me, "Do not weep! See, the Lion of the tribe of Judah, the Root of David, has triumphed. He is able to open the scroll and its seven seals."...
In a loud voice they sang:

"Worthy is the Lamb, who was slain,
to receive power and wealth and wisdom and strength
and honor and glory and praise!"

Then I heard every creature in heaven and on earth and under the earth and on the sea, and all that is in them, singing:

"To him who sits on the throne and to the Lamb
be praise and honor and glory and power,
for ever and ever!" **Revelation 5:5, 12-13**

... "Great and marvelous are your deeds,
Lord God Almighty.
Just and true are your ways,
King of the ages.
Who will not fear you, O Lord,
and bring glory to your name?
For you alone are holy.
All nations will come
and worship before you,
for your righteous acts have been revealed." **Revelation 15:3-4**

Let us rejoice and be glad
   and give him glory!
For the wedding of the Lamb has come,
   and his bride has made herself ready. **Revelation 19:7**

6

Agreement Brings Boldness

"THE WICKED MAN FLEES THOUGH NO ONE PURSUES, but the righteous are as bold as a lion" (Proverbs 28:1). *Bold as a lion.* That's what spiritual warriors are to be, especially when calling upon the Lord for help.

Jesus tells a parable about a persistent man who goes at midnight to ask his neighbor for three loaves of bread for unexpected company. He knocks. He knocks again. He keeps on knocking. He states a specific request. Finally, the reluctant neighbor gets up and gives him the desired three loaves (see Luke 11:5-13).

God is never reluctant to grant our requests. Rather this parable concerns asking for a specific need with unashamed boldness and persistence. Jesus says: "... yet because of his shameless persistence and insistence, he will get up and give him as much as he needs. So I say to you, ask and keep on asking, and it shall be given you; seek and keep on seeking, and you shall find; knock and keep on knocking, and the door shall be opened to you" (Luke 11:8b, 9 AMP).

Bible teacher Jack Hayford says of this parable:

> The lesson revolves around one idea: shameless boldness.... Boldness is your privilege. Your assignment is to ask; his commitment is to give—as much as you need.
>
> Too many hesitate to pray. They hesitate through a sense of unworthiness, a feeling of distance from deity, a wondering about God's will in the matter... a fear that God won't hear.... Jesus strikes the death blow to such hesitancy: ask. Ask with unabashed forwardness; ask with shameless boldness, he commands. And when you do, he clearly teaches, "your friend, my Father, will rise to the occasion and see that everything you need is provided."[1]

God wants us to cry out to him. He says through the prophet Jeremiah: "Call to Me and I will answer you and show you great and mighty things, fenced in and hidden, which you do not know—do not distinguish and recognize, have knowledge of and understand" (Jeremiah 33:3 AMP).

THE POWER OF AGREEMENT

Your private prayer is important and potent, but praying with a prayer partner strengthens your effectiveness. Jesus encouraged us: "Again, I tell you that if two of you on earth agree about anything you ask for, it will be done for you by my Father in heaven. For where two or three come together in my name, there am I with them" (Matthew 18:19-20).

The word "agree" in this Scripture derives from a Greek word from which we get our English word "symphony." It means "to be in accord or in harmony" or "to make one mind."

Jesus was always in agreement with his heavenly Father, never doing or saying anything except what the Father instructed. In like manner, we can ask the Lord for his mind about a situation or problem, then pray in agreement—or with one mind—with a prayer partner until we see results. Remember that battles aren't always won instantly; we must be persistent. And each battle requires a different strategy.

Ask the Lord for the right prayer support—be it one person or a team—who will agree in prayer with the way God has shown you to pray. Find partners who will remain steadfast and pray with you until victory is accomplished.

Here are two sample prayers of agreement from Scripture:

He has delivered us from such a deadly peril, and he will deliver us. On him we have set our hope that he will continue to deliver us, as you help us by your prayers.

2 Corinthians 1:10-11a

About midnight Paul and Silas were praying and singing hymns to God, and the other prisoners were listening to them. Suddenly there was such a violent earthquake that the foundations of the prison were shaken. At once all the prison doors flew open, and everybody's chains came loose.

Acts 16:25-26

ANGELIC INTERVENTION

Not only are we to pray boldly and in agreement, we can count on God to send heavenly reinforcements: angels. We see several accounts in Scripture:

2 Kings 6:17	Elisha's servant sees invisible chariots protecting them.
Psalm 34:6-7	An angel comes to the aid of David.
Psalm 91:11	God promises to "command his angels" to protect his child.
Daniel 6:22	An angel shuts the mouths of the lions and delivers Daniel.

Daniel 10:5-14   An angel brings the answer to Daniel's prayer, after encountering opposition with satanic "princes."

Thomas B. White, in *The Believers's Guide to Spiritual Warfare*, explains:

The connection between prayer and angelic operation did not cease in the early church. With Peter in prison (Acts 12), the church prayed earnestly, and an angel came to set the Apostle free. Acts 12:15 gives evidence of the possibility of guardian angels. There is a connection between the calling and the outworking of God's will. But we cannot know, nor should we try to find out, the extent to which the angels are dependent upon our prayers. That's God business, and he hasn't given us a lot of light on it. Our proper responsibility is to earnestly pray and trust God to work. Our confidence must be that when we pray in faith, the Lord hears and chooses the means through which he will work.[2]

We can ask the Lord to intervene with angels, but we do not personally have the right to command angels to do our bidding. Sometimes we may cry out in an emergency, "Lord, please dispatch your angels to protect our son in that blinding snowstorm! Thank you for his safety."

SCRIPTURES

Be self-controlled and alert. Your enemy the devil prowls around like a roaring lion looking for someone to devour. Resist him, standing firm in the faith, because you know that your brothers throughout the world are undergoing the same kind of sufferings.   1 Peter 5:8-9

Five of you will chase a hundred, and a hundred of you will chase ten thousand, and your enemies will fall by the sword before you.   Leviticus 26:8

Moses answered the people, "Do not be afraid. Stand firm and you will see the deliverance the LORD will bring you today. The Egyptians you see today you will never see again."

Exodus 14:13

Have I not commanded you? Be strong and courageous. Do not be terrified; do not be discouraged, for the LORD your God will be with you wherever you go. Joshua 1:9

The LORD said to Joshua, "Do not be afraid of them; I have given them into your hand. Not one of them will be able to withstand you." Joshua 10:8

The LORD has driven out before you great and powerful nations; to this day no one has been able to withstand you. One of you routs a thousand, because the LORD your God fights for you, just as he promised. So be very careful to love the LORD your God. Joshua 23:9-11

David said to the Philistine, "You come against me with sword and spear and javelin, but I come against you in the name of the LORD Almighty, the God of the armies of Israel, whom you have defied. This day the LORD will hand you over to me.... All those gathered here will know that it is not by sword or spear that the LORD saves; for the battle is the LORD's, and he will give all of you into our hands." 1 Samuel 17:45-47

It is God who arms me with strength
　and makes my way perfect.
He makes my feet like the feet of a deer;
　he enables me to stand on the heights.
He trains my hands for battle;
　my arms can bend a bow of bronze....
You armed me with strength for battle;
　you made my adversaries bow at my feet.
You made my enemies turn their backs in flight,
　and I destroyed my foes. 2 Samuel 22:33-35, 40-41

"Don't be afraid," the prophet answered. "Those who are with us are more than those who are with them."

And Elisha prayed, "O LORD, open his eyes so he may see." Then the LORD opened the servant's eyes, and he looked and saw the hills full of horses and chariots of fire all around Elisha. **2 Kings 6:16-17**

You will not have to fight this battle. Take up your positions; stand firm and see the deliverance the LORD will give you, O Judah and Jerusalem. Do not be afraid; do not be discouraged. Go out to face them tomorrow, and the LORD will be with you. **2 Chronicles 20:17**

"... the joy of the LORD is your strength." **Nehemiah 8:10**

You, O LORD, keep my lamp burning;
  my God turns my darkness into light.
With your help I can advance against a troop;
  with my God I can scale a wall. **Psalm 18:28-29**

Now I know that the LORD saves his anointed;
  he answers him from his holy heaven
  with the saving power of his right hand.
Some trust in chariots and some in horses,
  but we trust in the name of the LORD our God.
They are brought to their knees and fall,
  but we rise up and stand firm. **Psalm 20:6-8**

When the storm has swept by, the wicked are gone,
  but the righteous stand firm forever. **Proverbs 10:25**

Strengthen the feeble hands,
  steady the knees that give way;
say to those with fearful hearts,
  "Be strong, do not fear;
your God will come,
  he will come with vengeance;

with divine retribution
he will come to save you." **Isaiah 35:3-4**

"I am the LORD, the God of all mankind. Is anything too hard for me?..." **Jeremiah 32:27**

... but the people who know their God shall prove themselves strong and shall stand firm, and do exploits [for God].

Daniel 11:32 AMP

After this the Lord appointed seventy-two others and sent them two by two ahead of him to every town and place where he was about to go. He told them, "The harvest is plentiful, but the workers are few. Ask the Lord of the harvest, therefore, to send out workers into his harvest field. Go! I am sending you out like lambs among wolves...." **Luke 10:1-3**

"But you will receive power when the Holy Spirit comes on you; and you will be my witnesses in Jerusalem, and in all Judea and Samaria, and to the ends of the earth." **Acts 1:8**

I appeal to you, brothers, in the name of our Lord Jesus Christ, that all of you agree with one another so that there may be no divisions among you and that you may be perfectly united in mind and thought. **1 Corinthians 1:10**

Therefore, my dear brothers, stand firm. Let nothing move you. Always give yourselves fully to the work of the Lord, because you know that your labor in the Lord is not in vain.... Be on your guard; stand firm in the faith; be men of courage; be strong. **1 Corinthians 15:58; 16:13**

Let us not become weary in doing good, for at the proper time we will reap a harvest if we do not give up. **Galatians 6:9**

Because of my chains, most of the brothers in the Lord have been encouraged to speak the word of God more courageously and fearlessly. **Philippians 1:14**

Submit yourselves, then, to God. Resist the devil, and he will flee from you.... Be patient and stand firm, because the Lord's coming is near. James 4:7; 5:8

But the Lord stood at my side and gave me strength, so that through me the message might be fully proclaimed and all the Gentiles might hear it. And I was delivered from the lion's mouth. The Lord will rescue me from every evil attack and will bring me safely to his heavenly kingdom.... 2 Timothy 4:17-18

Not that we are competent in ourselves to claim anything for ourselves, but our competence comes from God.... Therefore, since we have such a hope, we are very bold.... And we, who with unveiled faces all reflect the Lord's glory, are being transformed into his likeness with ever-increasing glory, which comes from the Lord, who is the Spirit.

Therefore, since through God's mercy we have this ministry, we do not lose heart. 2 Corinthians 3:5, 12, 18; 4:1

A PRAYER OF AGREEMENT

Lord, thank you that I can come fearlessly, boldly, confidently to you in prayer. Reveal to me things which I need to know and understand that I might pray what is on your heart. Purify my heart so I will ask with the right motive, confident that you want to answer.

Lord, help me always to pray in harmony with your will. Link me up with the right prayer partner(s) who will stand in agreement, calling forth your plans and purposes. Thank you for the privilege of prayer! I give you praise in Jesus' name. Amen.

7

Other Strategies for Battle

W E NOW TURN OUR ATTENTION to four other effective strategies in spiritual warfare: fasting, weeping, laughter, and shouts of joy. Experienced intercessors readily attest to the value of all four. Depending on what God wants to accomplish through us during that particular time of intercession, the Holy Spirit can guide us as to when to use each specific tool.

FASTING

Abstaining from food is a physical act, but one which has spiritual significance as well. Coupled with prayer, it can be a powerful weapon in spiritual warfare. Once when the disciples could not cure a child suffering from seizures, Jesus told them it was due to their unbelief. Then he added, "... this kind does not go out except by prayer and fasting" (Matthew 17:21 NKJV).

Jesus himself fasted prior to momentous events in his ministry. He made it clear he expected his followers to fast as well: "When you fast, do not look somber as the hypocrites do, for they disfigure their faces to show men they are fasting. I tell you the truth, they have received their reward in full. But when you fast, put oil on your head and wash your face, so that it will not be obvious to men that you are fasting, but only to your Father, who is unseen; and your Father, who sees what is done in secret, will reward you" (Matthew 6:16-18).

John's disciples chided Jesus because his disciples did not fast. He replied that as long as the bridegroom was with them, they need not fast. But when Jesus was taken away, then his followers would fast (see Matthew 9:14-15). That certainly includes us today.

We see many other examples of fasting in the Bible:

David	2 Samuel 12:16; Psalm 109:24
Nehemiah	Nehemiah 1:4
Esther	Esther 4:16
Daniel	Daniel 9:3
John's disciples	Matthew 9:14-15
Anna	Luke 2:37
Cornelius	Acts 13:2
Paul	2 Corinthians 11:27

Why fast? Scripture answers:

> Is not this the kind of fasting I [God] have chosen:
>   to loose the chains of injustice
> and untie the cords of the yoke,
>   to set the oppressed free and break every yoke?
>
> **Isaiah 58:6**

In addition to setting free the oppressed, fasting and prayer can also yield direction and answers from God, strategy for warfare, new revelation of Scripture, a closer walk with the Lord, a humbling of self, healing, and deliverance from evil spirits.

In his book *God's Chosen Fast*, Arthur Wallis states:

We must not think of fasting as a hunger strike designed to force God's hand and get our own way! Prayer, however, is more complex than simply asking a loving father to supply his child's needs. Prayer is warfare. Prayer is wrestling. There are opposing forces. There are spiritual cross currents.

... The man who prays with fasting is giving heaven notice that he is truly in earnest; that he will not give up nor let God go without the blessing.[1]

When you fast, be sure to pray and read Scripture. Allow time for God to speak to you, either through the Word, or by the still, small voice of the Holy Spirit whispering in your heart.

If for health reasons you cannot go on an extended fast, you can try a modified fast. Or you can give up a favorite food as an act of denying yourself during a specific period set aside for prayer. Start with one-day to three-day fasts before attempting a prolonged period, and drink lots of water or diluted clear juices while fasting. The motive of the heart behind the fasting is more important than the length of the fast. The important thing is openness and obedience to the voice of the Holy Spirit.

Expect opposition from Satan when you enter a fast. He attacked Jesus in the wilderness and tempted him to turn stones into bread after his forty days without food. Ask God for strength to overcome attacks of weakness, exaggerated hunger pangs, nausea, or headaches. Just as Jesus answered the tempter by quoting the Word of God, so can we. "... Man does not live on bread alone, but on every word that comes from the mouth of God" (Matthew 4:4).

A COLLECTIVE FAST

Once when the people of Judah were suffering under God's judgment for disobedience, he told Joel to call the people to fasting and repentance:

"Declare a holy fast;
    call a sacred assembly.
Summon the elders
    and all who live in the land
to the house of the LORD your God,
    and cry out to the LORD."   Joel 1:14

"Even now," declares the LORD,
    "return to me with all your heart,
    with fasting and weeping and mourning."
Rend your heart
    and not your garments.
Return to the LORD your God,
    for he is gracious and compassionate,
slow to anger and abounding in love,
    and he relents from sending calamity.
Who knows? He may turn and have pity
    and leave behind a blessing—
grain offerings and drink offerings
    for the LORD your God.
Blow the trumpet in Zion,
    declare a holy fast,
call a sacred assembly.   Joel 2:12-15

"I [the Lord] will repay you for the years the locusts have
        eaten....
You will have plenty to eat, until you are full,
    and you will praise the name of the LORD your God,
who has worked wonders for you;
    never again will my people be shamed.   Joel 2:25a, 26

The prophet Daniel recorded his experience with fasting:

So I turned to the Lord God and pleaded with him in
prayer and petition, in fasting, and in sackcloth and ashes.
... While I was speaking and praying, confessing my sin and
the sin of my people Israel and making my request to the
LORD... Gabriel, the man I had seen in the earlier vision,

came to me in swift flight about the time of the evening sacrifice. He instructed me and said to me, "Daniel, I have now come to give you insight and understanding."

Daniel 9:3, 20-22

A PRAYER FOR FASTING

Lord, help me heed your call to fast and pray and seek your direction. I know fasting can accomplish much in me as well as in the situation or people for whom I'm interceding. I need your direction for how long to fast and your strength to do it. My spirit is willing but my body often frail. Give me your wisdom, Lord, and help me to glorify you through my fasting. In Jesus' name, Amen.

WEEPING

God promises:

Those who sow in tears
   will reap with songs of joy.
He who goes out weeping,
   carrying seed to sow,
will return with songs of joy,
   carrying sheaves with him.   **Psalm 126:5-6**

Dick Eastman, popular teacher on prayer and intercession, comments on this psalm:

Tears in Scripture play a unique role in spiritual breakthrough. Here we discover that the planting of seeds accompanied by a spirit of brokenness will not only bring a spiritual harvest of results, but will leave the sower with a spirit of rejoicing in the process. This passage, along with numerous others in Scripture regarding a spirit of brokenness, pictures a variety of purposes and functions related to what might be termed "the ministry of tears," a ministry Charles H. Spurgeon defined as "liquid prayer."

Eastman goes on to mention six different types of tears:

1. Tears of sorrow or suffering (2 Kings 20:5)
2. Tears of joy (Genesis 33:4)
3. Tears of compassion (John 11:35)
4. Tears of desperation (Esther 4:1, 3)
5. Tears of travail (Isaiah 42:14)
6. Tears of repentance (Joel 2:12, 13)[2]

In our quiet times with the Lord, we may find ourselves weeping or in travail as we pray. Our weeping could be due to any of the above reasons. The psalmist David once prayed:

"Record my lament;
   list my tears on your scroll—
   are they not in your record?
Then my enemies will turn back
   when I call for help.
By this I will know that God is for me." **Psalm 56:8-9**

SCRIPTURES ON WEEPING

This is what the LORD Almighty says:
   "Consider now! Call for the wailing women to come;
      send for the most skillful of them.
   Let them come quickly
      and wail over us
   till our eyes overflow with tears
      and water streams from our eyelids.
   The sound of wailing is heard from Zion...." **Jeremiah 9:17-19**

Streams of tears flow from my eyes,
   for your law is not obeyed. **Psalm 119:136**

… The Sovereign LORD will wipe away the tears
    from all faces;
he will remove the disgrace of his people
    from all the earth.
The LORD has spoken.   **Isaiah 25:8**

Oh, that my head were a spring of water
    and my eyes a fountain of tears!
I would weep day and night
    for the slain of my people.   **Jeremiah 9:1**

But if you do not listen,
    I will weep in secret because of your pride;
my eyes will weep bitterly,
    overflowing with tears,
because the LORD's flock will be taken captive.   **Jeremiah 13:17**

This is what the LORD says:

    "Restrain your voice from weeping
        and your eyes from tears,
    for your work will be rewarded,"
        declares the LORD.
    "They will return from the land of the enemy."
                                      Jeremiah 31:16

"This is why I weep
    and my eyes overflow with tears.
No one is near to comfort me,
    no one to restore my spirit.
My children are destitute
    because the enemy has prevailed."   **Lamentations 1:16**

Let the priests, who minister before the LORD,
    weep between the temple porch and the altar.
Let them say, "Spare your people, O LORD.
    Do not make your inheritance an object of scorn,
    a byword among the nations.

Why should they say among the peoples,
   'Where is their God?"   Joel 2:17

"Blessed are those who mourn,
   for they will be comforted."   Matthew 5:4

Rejoice with those who rejoice; mourn with those who mourn.   Romans 12:15

For I wrote you out of great distress and anguish of heart and with many tears, not to grieve you but to let you know the depth of my love for you.   2 Corinthians 2:4

... I am happy... because your sorrow led you to repentance.... Godly sorrow brings repentance that leads to salvation and leaves no regret, but worldy sorrow brings death.
   2 Corinthians 7:9-10

During the days of Jesus' life on earth, he offered up prayers and petitions with loud cries and tears to the one who could save him from death, and he was heard because of his reverent submission.   Hebrews 5:7

Come near to God and he will come near to you. Wash your hands, you sinners, and purify your hearts, you double-minded. Grieve, mourn and wail. Change your laughter to mourning and your joy to gloom. Humble yourselves before the Lord, and he will lift you up.   James 4:8-10

Then one of the elders said to me, "Do not weep! See, the Lion of the tribe of Judah, the Root of David, has triumphed. He is able to open the scroll and its seven seals."   Revelation 5:5

A PRAYER FOR WEEPING

   Lord, you see my tears as I identify with the hurting, lost ones for whom I intercede. Please give me a heart of compassion. Help me to be able to pray with discernment and wisdom for the ones you put on my heart. Receive my tears as intercession for their deepest needs. In Jesus' name, Amen.

LAUGHTER

Laughter may seem a strange warfare strategy. When we can laugh in spite of what the enemy is trying to put upon us, we'll quickly put him to flight. Most of the biblical references to laughter mean "to mock, to make sport, to deride, to laugh, to scorn"—a very appropriate stance toward Satan.

When a powerful king of Assyria threatened to conquer all the land of Judah, King Hezekiah prayed for deliverance and asked God to vindicate his name. The Lord responded through the prophet Isaiah with this word: "This is the word that the LORD has spoken against him [the king of Assyria]:

'The Virgin Daughter of Zion
    despises you and mocks you.
The Daughter of Jerusalem
    tosses her head as you flee.
Who is it you have insulted and blasphemed?
Against whom have you raised your voice
    and lifted your eyes in pride?
Against the Holy One of Israel!'" **2 Kings 19:21-22**

The Holy Spirit may direct spiritual warriors to laugh in scorn at the devil's plan. An African proverb says, "When a mouse laughs at a cat, there must be a hole nearby." The enemy may seem bigger and stronger than we are, but we can rely on God's almighty power to deliver us. Bible teacher Gwen Shaw comments, "If we are to allow God to laugh, then he must laugh through us, just as he speaks through us."[3]

"God named Abraham's son Isaac, which means laughter," a pastor notes, "and the Bible often refers to Jehovah as the God of Isaac (laughter). When Abraham first heard the promise that he'd have a son though he was a hundred years old, he fell down laughing [Genesis 17:17]. Not just a chuckle. It was Holy Spirit 'belly laughter.'"

Sarah also laughed to herself as she thought, "After I am worn out and my master is old, will I now have this pleasure?" (Genesis 18:12). "God has brought me laughter, and everyone who hears about this will laugh with me" (Genesis 21:6).

SCRIPTURES ON SCORNFUL LAUGHTER

The One enthroned in heaven laughs;
  the LORD scoffs at them. **Psalm 2:4**

The wicked plot against the righteous
  and gnash their teeth at them;
but the LORD laughs at the wicked,
  for he knows their day is coming. **Psalm 37:12-13**

The righteous will see and fear;
  they will laugh at him, saying,
"Here now is the man
  who did not make God his stronghold
but trusted in his great wealth
  and grew strong by destroying others!" **Psalm 52:6-7**

See what they [wicked nations] spew from their mouths—
  they spew out swords from their lips,
  and they say, "Who can hear us?"
But you, O LORD, laugh at them;
  you scoff at all those nations. **Psalm 59:7-8**

JOYFUL LAUGHTER

Still other definitions of laughter include: "a mark of gratification" and "joy restored." Paul wrote, "Rejoice in the Lord always. I will say it again: Rejoice!" (Philippians 4:4). Examples of women in the Bible who rejoiced are Miriam (Exodus 15:20-21), Hannah (1 Samuel 2:1-10), and Mary (Luke 1:46-55).

He will yet fill your mouth with laughter
   and your lips with shouts of joy.
Your enemies will be clothed in shame,
   and the tents of the wicked will be no more.   **Job 8:21-22**

A cheerful heart is good medicine,
but a crushed spirit dries up the bones.   **Proverbs 17:22**

There is a time for everything,
and a season for every activity under heaven:
... a time to weep and a time to laugh,
a time to mourn and a time to dance....   **Ecclesiastes 3:1, 4**

Blessed are you who hunger now,
   for you will be satisfied.
Blessed are you who weep now,
   for you will laugh.   **Luke 6:21**

SHOUTS OF JOY

A shout can be anything from an acclamation of joy to a battle cry. It can be a crying noise, a crashing sound, loud clamor, a cry of excitement. Jesus himself will return with a shout or a word of command (see 1 Thessalonians 4:16).

SCRIPTURES ON SHOUTING

The walls of Jericho collapsed when the Israelites marched around them seven times in one day, then shouted at Joshua's command: "Shout! For the Lord has given you the city!" (see Joshua 6:16).

And on that day they offered great sacrifices, rejoicing because God had given them great joy. The women and children also rejoiced. The sound of rejoicing in Jerusalem could be heard far away.   **Nehemiah 12:43**

We will shout for joy when you are victorious
     and will lift up our banners in the name of our God.
May the LORD grant all your requests.   **Psalm 20:5**

Then my head will be exalted
     above the enemies who surround me;
     at his tabernacle will I sacrifice with shouts of joy;
I will sing and make music to the LORD.   **Psalm 27:6**

You turned my wailing into dancing;
you removed my sackcloth and clothed me with joy....
                                        Psalm 30:11

Sing to him a new song;
     play skillfully, and shout for joy.   **Psalm 33:3**

Come, let us sing for joy to the LORD;
     let us shout aloud to the Rock of our salvation.   **Psalm 95:1**

with trumpets and the blast of the ram's horn—
     shout for joy before the LORD, the King.   **Psalm 98:6**

He brought out his people with rejoicing,
     his chosen ones with shouts of joy....   **Psalm 105:43**

Shouts of joy and victory
     resound in the tents of the righteous:
"The LORD's right hand has done mighty things!"
                                        Psalm 118:15

Our mouths were filled with laughter,
     our tongues with songs of joy.
Then it was said among the nations,
"The LORD has done great things for them."   **Psalm 126:2**

They raise their voices, they shout for joy;
     from the west they acclaim the LORD's majesty.   **Isaiah 24:14**

PRAYER FOR LAUGHTER

Lord, thank you for the gift of laughter. Thank you that even you laugh. Show us when to laugh at the enemy in our warfare as you bring deliverance through your mighty hand and outstretched arm. Thank you for the times when we can shout for joy and take spoils from the enemy. We praise you in Jesus' name. Amen.

8

Assured of Victory

SPIRITUAL WARRIORS NEED to remind themselves and the enemy that his defeat is an irreversible fact. This is best done by wielding the proclamations of God's Word against our adversary, whose ruin is sealed. Arthur Mathews affirms:

> Satan is a defeated foe, with a crushed head. There is no power in him, nor are there any means available to him to reach and unseat the Victor of Calvary now seated at the right hand of the Father.
>
> It is not for us to fight *for* victory.... Our fight is *from* victory; and from this vantage point, empowered with Christ's might, and completely enclosed in the whole armor of God, the powers of evil are compelled to back off as we resist them.[1]

Scripture encourages us to look beyond the difficult or seemingly impossible circumstances which Satan often uses to weaken our faith. We must fix our spiritual eyes on Jesus— "the author and perfecter of our faith" (Hebrews 12:2)—who secures the victory. By believing God instead of the lies of the enemy, we cooperate with his plan for victory and confound the enemy's plan. Our faith, anchored in God's Word, need not be shaken by circumstances.

Puritan author William Gurnall wrote:

> I am not to believe what the Word says merely because it agrees with my reason; but I must believe my reason because it aligns with the Word. A carpenter lays his rule to the plank and sees it to be straight or crooked; yet it is not the eye but the rule that is the measure. He can always trust his rule to be right.[2]

Our assurance of victory over Satan is based upon the integrity and infallibility of God's Word, not upon our own interpretation of circumstances. Use the following verses of Scripture to verbally declare your faith in God's promise, and in his power to fulfill that promise. Your declaration of victory will push back the enemy and immobilize his attack.

SCRIPTURES DECLARING GOD'S PROMISES

... the LORD was gracious to Sarah as he had said, and the LORD did for Sarah what he had promised.   **Genesis 21:1**

I will send my terror ahead of you and throw into confusion every nation you encounter. I will make all your enemies turn their backs and run.   **Exodus 23:27**

For the LORD your God is the one who goes with you to fight for you against your enemies to give you victory....

The LORD will grant that the enemies who rise up against you will be defeated before you. They will come at you from one direction but flee from you in seven.   **Deuteronomy 20:4; 28:7**

The eternal God is your refuge,
    and underneath are the everlasting arms.
He will drive out your enemy before you,
    saying, "Destroy him!"   **Deuteronomy 33:27**

The LORD will march out like a mighty man,
    like a warrior he will stir up his zeal;
with a shout he will raise the battle cry
    and will triumph over his enemies.   **Isaiah 42:13**

"... no weapon forged against you will prevail,
    and you will refute every tongue that accuses you.
This is the heritage of the servants of the LORD,
    and this is their vindication from me,"
declares the LORD.   **Isaiah 54:17**

Before they call I will answer;
    while they are still speaking I will hear.   **Isaiah 65:24**

"... nothing is impossible with God."
"Blessed is she who has believed that what the Lord has said to
her will be accomplished!"   **Luke 1:37, 45**

"If you remain in me and my words remain in you, ask whatever you wish, and it will be given you. This is to my Father's glory, that you bear much fruit, showing yourselves to be my disciples."   **John 15:7-8**

For [Christ] must reign until he has put all his enemies under his feet. The last enemy to be destroyed is death....
    ... then the saying that is written will come true: "Death has been swallowed up in victory."
    "Where, O death, is your victory?
        Where, O death, is your sting?"
    The sting of death is sin, and the power of sin is the law. But thanks be to God! He gives us the victory through our Lord Jesus Christ.   **1 Corinthians 15:25-26, 54-56**

SCRIPTURES DECLARING GOD'S POWER

... he [Abraham] faced the fact that his body was as good as dead... and that Sarah's womb was also dead. Yet he did not waver through unbelief regarding the promise of God, but was strengthened in his faith and gave glory to God, being fully persuaded that God had power to do what he had promised.   **Romans 4:19-21**

"Your right hand, O LORD,
   was majestic in power.
Your right hand, O LORD,
   shattered the enemy....
The enemy boasted,
   'I will pursue, I will overtake them.
I will divide the spoils;
   I will gorge myself on them.
I will draw my sword
   and my hand will destroy them.'
But you blew with your breath,
   and the sea covered them.
They sank like lead
   in the mighty waters...."   **Exodus 15:6, 9-10**

... the Lord brought us out of Egypt with a mighty hand and an outstretched arm, with great terror and with miraculous signs and wonders.   **Deuteronomy 26:8**

He rebuked the Red Sea, and it dried up;
   he led them through the depths as through a desert.
He saved them from the hand of the foe;
   from the hand of the enemy he redeemed them.
The waters covered their adversaries;
   not one of them survived.
Then they believed his promises
   and sang his praise.   **Psalm 106:9-12**

"To whom will you compare me?
Or who is my equal?" says the Holy One.

Lift your eyes and look to the heavens:
  Who created all these?
He who brings out the starry host one by one,
  and calls them each by name.
Because of his great power and mighty strength,
  not one of them is missing.... **Isaiah 40:25-26**

"... I am the LORD,
who has made all things,
who alone stretched out the heavens,
who spread out the earth by myself,
who foils the signs of false prophets
  and makes fools of diviners,
who overthrows the learning of the wise
  and turns it into nonsense,
who carries out the words of his servants
  and fulfills the predictions of his messengers...." **Isaiah 44:24-26**

... that the eyes of your heart may be enlightened in order that you may know... his incomparably great power for us who believe. That power is like the working of his mighty strength, which he exerted in Christ when he raised him from the dead and seated him at his right hand in the heavenly realms, far above all rule and authority, power and dominion, and every title that can be given, not only in the present age but also in the one to come. And God placed all things under his feet and appointed him to be head over everything for the church.... **Ephesians 1:18-22**

... God made you alive with Christ. He forgave us all our sins, having canceled the written code, with its regulations, that was against us and that stood opposed to us; he took it away, nailing it to the cross. And having disarmed the powers and authorities, he made a public spectacle of them, triumphing over them by the cross. **Colossians 2:13-15**

I am the Living One; I was dead, and behold I am alive for ever and ever! And I hold the keys of death and Hades.
  Revelation 1:18

SCRIPTURES DECLARING GOD'S JUSTICE

"... Will not the Judge of all the earth do right?" **Genesis 18:25**

... those who oppose the LORD will be shattered.
He will thunder against them from heaven;
   the LORD will judge the ends of the earth.... **1 Samuel 2:10**

"... Now let the fear of the LORD be upon you. Judge carefully,
for with the LORD our God there is no injustice or partiality or
bribery." **2 Chronicles 19:7**

He will judge the world in righteousness;
   he will govern the peoples with justice. **Psalm 9:8**

Your throne, O God, will last for ever and ever;
   a scepter of justice will be the scepter of your kingdom.

Psalm 45:6

Say among the nations, "The LORD reigns."
The world is firmly established, it cannot be moved;
   he will judge the peoples with equity. **Psalm 96:10**

For God will bring every deed into judgment,
   including every hidden thing,
whether it is good or evil. **Ecclesiastes 12:14**

... and he [Messiah] will delight in the fear of the LORD.
He will not judge by what he sees with his eyes,
   or decide by what he hears with his ears;
but with righteousness he will judge the needy,
   with justice he will give decisions for the poor of the earth.
He will strike the earth with the rod of his mouth;
   with the breath of his lips he will slay the wicked. **Isaiah 11:3-4**

... he will swallow up death forever.
The Sovereign LORD will wipe away the tears
   from all faces;

he will remove the disgrace of his people
    from all the earth.
The LORD has spoken.   Isaiah 25:8

Yet the LORD longs to be gracious to you;
    he rises to show you compassion.
For the LORD is a God of justice.
Blessed are all who wait for him!   Isaiah 30:18

God presented him [Jesus] as a sacrifice of atonement,
through faith in his blood. He did this to demonstrate his
justice....   Romans 3:25

... "See, the Lord is coming with thousands upon thousands
of his holy ones to judge everyone, and to convict all the
ungodly of all the ungodly acts they have done in the ungodly
way, and of all the harsh words ungodly sinners have spoken
against him."   Jude 14-15

CONFESSIONS OF VICTORY

It was not by their sword that they won the land,
    nor did their arm bring them victory;
it was your right hand, your arm,
    and the light of your face, for you loved them....
I do not trust in my bow,
    my sword does not bring me victory;
but you give us victory over our enemies,
    you put our adversaries to shame.
In God we make our boast all day long,
    and we will praise your name forever.   Psalm 44:3, 6-8

He ransoms me unharmed
    from the battle waged against me,
    even though many oppose me....
With God we will gain the victory,
    and he will trample down our enemies.   Psalms 55:18; 60:12

Your arm is endued with power;
   your hand is strong, your right hand exalted.
Righteousness and justice are the foundation of your throne;
   love and faithfulness go before you.   **Psalm 89:13-14**

Do not gloat over me, my enemy!
Though I have fallen, I will rise.
Though I sit in darkness,
   the LORD will be my light....
Then my enemy will see it
   and will be covered with shame,
she who said to me,
   "Where is the LORD your God?"
My eyes will see her downfall;
   even now she will be trampled underfoot
like mire in the streets.   **Micah 7:8, 10**

But thanks be to God! He gives us the victory through our Lord Jesus Christ.   **1 Corinthians 15:57**

But thanks be to God, who always leads us in triumphal procession in Christ and through us spreads everywhere the fragrance of the knowledge of him.   **2 Corinthians 2:14**

... for everyone born of God overcomes the world. This is the victory that has overcome the world, even our faith. Who is it that overcomes the world? Only he who believes that Jesus is the Son of God....

   This is the confidence we have in approaching God: that if we ask anything according to his will, he hears us. And if we know that he hears us—whatever we ask—we know that we have what we asked of him....

   We know that anyone born of God does not continue to sin; the one who was born of God keeps him safe, and the evil one cannot harm him.   **1 John 5:4-5, 14-15, 18**

PART TWO

Winning Your Personal Battles

9

Assurance of Salvation

SATAN CONSTANTLY ACCUSES US before God (see Revelation 12:9-10). Our enemy seeks to destroy our confidence in Christ by causing us to doubt our salvation. Many Christians suffer great mental anguish over the question, "How can I know whether I'm truly born again?" Their sense of unworthiness and guilt often drive them to try to "earn" salvation through good works or penance. Or they completely give up on trying to be a Christian, feeling they can never "meet the qualifications."

This reaction actually cooperates with Satan's desire to nullify the power of Christ's sacrificial death, burial, and resurrection. If it were possible to *earn* salvation, we wouldn't need a savior!

God's Word clearly teaches that we are reborn by confessing our sins, declaring our faith in Christ, and receiving forgiveness and cleansing through his grace. The transaction occurs instantly. However, growing into maturity and exhibiting the fruits of the Spirit require time and patience in learning Scripture and applying it to our lives.

T.W. Wilson explains the meaning of atonement:

> The Old Testament Hebrew word that we translate "atonement" means literally "to cover up." The animal sacrifices were intended to "cover" a man's sins. In the New Testament, however, the meaning of atoning sacrifice is conveyed by the word "expiate," which means "to put away." The blood that Jesus shed in our behalf on the cross at Calvary does not merely cover up our sin, it puts away our sin as though it had never been committed.[1]

When you stumble and fall in your walk with the Lord (as Peter did), you can repent and get on your feet again. Don't believe the lie that God has rejected you! When the enemy bombards your mind with doubt, use the following verses to proclaim your salvation.

SCRIPTURES

So the LORD God said to the serpent,
"… And I will put enmity
between you and the woman,
and between your offspring and hers;
he will crush your head,
and you will strike his heel."   **Genesis 3:14-15**

The LORD is my light and my salvation—
whom shall I fear?
The LORD is the stronghold of my life—
of whom shall I be afraid?   **Psalm 27:1**

We have sinned, even as our fathers did;
we have done wrong and acted wickedly.…

Yet he saved them for his name's sake,
  to make his mighty power known....
He saved them from the hand of the foe;
  from the hand of the enemy he redeemed them.

Psalm 106:6, 8, 10

In that day they will say,
"Surely this is our God;
  we trusted in him, and he saved us.
This is the LORD, we trusted in him;
  let us rejoice and be glad in his salvation." **Isaiah 25:9**

... my salvation will last forever,
  my righteousness will never fail ...
my righteousness will last forever,
  my salvation through all generations." **Isaiah 51:6, 8**

We all, like sheep, have gone astray,
  each of us has turned to his own way;
and the LORD has laid on him the iniquity of us all....
After the suffering of his soul,
  he will see the light [of life] and be satisfied;
by his knowledge my righteous servant will justify many,
  and he will bear their iniquities. **Isaiah 53:6, 11**

"All men will hate you because of me, but he who stands firm
to the end will be saved....
  "Whoever believes and is baptized will be saved, but whoever does not believe will be condemned." **Mark 13:13; 16:16**

"... do not rejoice that the spirits submit to you, but rejoice
that your names are written in heaven....
  "For the Son of Man came to seek and to save what was lost."

Luke 10:20; 19:10

For God so loved the world that he gave his one and only Son,
that whoever believes in him shall not perish but have eternal

life. For God did not send his Son into the world to condemn the world, but to save the world through him. **John 3:16-17**

"I tell you the truth, whoever hears my word and believes him who sent me has eternal life and will not be condemned; he has crossed over from death to life." **John 5:24**

"Then you will know the truth, and the truth will set you free....

"So if the Son sets you free, you will be free indeed."

John 8:32, 36

"I am the gate; whoever enters through me will be saved....

"I give them eternal life, and they shall never perish; no one can snatch them out of my hand." **John 10:9, 28**

... everyone who calls
     on the name of the Lord will be saved....
Salvation is found in no one else, for there is no other name under heaven given to men by which we must be saved.

Acts 2:21; 4:12

I am not ashamed of the gospel, because it is the power of God for the salvation of everyone who believes.... **Romans 1:16**

But now a righteousness from God, apart from law, has been made known....

This righteousness from God comes through faith in Jesus Christ to all who believe. There is no difference, for all have sinned and fall short of the glory of God, and are justified freely by his grace through the redemption that came by Christ Jesus. **Romans 3:21-24**

But now that you have been set free from sin and have become slaves to God, the benefit you reap leads to holiness, and the result is eternal life. For the wages of sin is death, but the gift of God is eternal life in Christ Jesus our Lord.

Romans 6:22-23

Therefore, there is now no condemnation for those who are in Christ Jesus, because through Christ Jesus the law of the Spirit of life set me free from the law of sin and death.

Romans 8:1-2

… if you confess with your mouth, "Jesus is Lord," and believe in your heart that God raised him from the dead, you will be saved. For it is with your heart that you believe and are justified, and it is with your mouth that you confess and are saved.

Romans 10:9-10

For the message of the cross is foolishness to those who are perishing, but to us who are being saved it is the power of God. **1 Corinthians 1:18**

Therefore, if anyone is in Christ, he is a new creation; the old has gone, the new has come! **2 Corinthians 5:17**

I have been crucified with Christ and I no longer live, but Christ lives in me. The life I live in the body, I live by faith in the Son of God, who loved me and gave himself for me.

Galatians 2:20

Clearly no one is justified before God by the law, because, "The righteous will live by faith." … Christ redeemed us from the curse of the law by becoming a curse for us, for it is written: "Cursed is everyone who is hung on a tree." **Galatians 3:11, 13**

But because of his great love for us, God, who is rich in mercy, made us alive with Christ even when we were dead in transgressions.… And God raised us up with Christ and seated us with him in the heavenly realms in Christ Jesus, in order that in the coming ages he might show the incomparable riches of his grace, expressed in his kindness to us in Christ Jesus. For it is by grace you have been saved, through faith—and this not from yourselves, it is the gift of God—not by works, so that no one can boast. **Ephesians 2:4-9**

... God our Savior... wants all men to be saved and to come to a knowledge of the truth.   1 Timothy 2:3-4

... This grace was given us in Christ Jesus before the beginning of time, but it has now been revealed through the appearing of our Savior, Christ Jesus, who has destroyed death and has brought life and immortality to light through the gospel.   2 Timothy 1:9-10

[He] gave himself for us to redeem us from all wickedness and to purify for himself a people that are his very own, eager to do what is good....

... he saved us, not because of righteous things we had done, but because of his mercy. He saved us through the washing of rebirth and renewal by the Holy Spirit....

Titus 2:14; 3:5

In bringing many sons to glory, it was fitting that God, for whom and through whom everything exists, should make the author of their salvation perfect through suffering....

... and, once made perfect, he became the source of eternal salvation for all who obey him....   Hebrews 2:10; 5:9

... because Jesus lives forever, he has a permanent priesthood. Therefore he is able to save completely those who come to God through him, because he always lives to intercede for them.

Such a high priest meets our need—one who is holy, blameless, pure, set apart from sinners, exalted above the heavens. Unlike the other high priests, he does not need to offer sacrifices day after day, first for his own sins, and then for the sins of the people. He sacrificed for their sins once for all when he offered himself.   Hebrews 7:24-27

Therefore, brothers, since we have confidence to enter the Most Holy Place by the blood of Jesus, by a new and living way opened for us through the curtain, that is, his body, and since

we have a great priest over the house of God, let us draw near
to God with a sincere heart in full assurance of faith, having
our hearts sprinkled to cleanse us from a guilty conscience
and having our bodies washed with pure water. Let us hold
unswervingly to the hope we profess, for he who promised is
faithful. **Hebrews 10:19-23**

If we confess our sins, he is faithful and just and will forgive us
our sins and purify us from all unrighteousness. **1 John 1:9**

... In his great mercy he has given us new birth into a living
hope through the resurrection of Jesus Christ from the dead,
and into an inheritance that can never perish, spoil or fade—
kept in heaven for you.... **1 Peter 1:3-4**

After this I heard what sounded like the roar of a great multitude in heaven shouting:
    "Hallelujah!
    Salvation and glory and power belong to our God...."
... Then I heard what sounded like a great multitude, like the
roar of rushing waters and like loud peals of thunder, shouting:
    "Hallelujah!
    For our Lord God Almighty reigns.
    Let us rejoice and be glad
       and give him glory!
    For the wedding of the Lamb has come,
       and his bride has made herself ready.
    Fine linen, bright and clean,
       was given her to wear...." **Revelation 19:1, 6-8**

A PRAYER OF ASSURANCE

Father, thank you that when Jesus shed his blood on the
cross he provided a way for my sins to be covered. I reaffirm
my faith in you and give you praise for the gift of salvation.

Thank you that I don't have to earn it. I accept Jesus' sacrifice for me and receive your forgiveness and cleansing. I rejoice in knowing I am your child, Father. Help me to obey your Word and daily acknowledge the Lordship of Jesus in my life. In his name, Amen.

10

Overcoming Depression and Burnout

DEPRESSION AND BURNOUT ARE TO THE MIND what sickness and disease are to the body. This emotional malady is a growing problem in the wake of modern society's relentless pursuit for success and achievement. Psychologist and author Dr. Archibald Hart observes:

> A culture such as ours, where there is a high priority placed on performance and success as symbols of worthiness and where there is a diminishing opportunity to be successful, is bound to give rise to an increased gap between expectations and accomplishments. This in turn creates disillusionment....
>
> ... Equally important is the increasing abuse and misuse of the body. *Stress* is the key word explaining this abuse. The

more complex a culture, the greater is the experience of stress. The consequent physiological distress plays havoc with the biochemical processes of the body, and depression is a symptom and the natural outcome of this distress.[1]

Some cases of depression may be caused by an imbalance in the body's chemistry, side-effects of medication, or insufficient nutrition. Usually a combination of physical, emotional, and spiritual factors come into play. Sinful attitudes and actions, and subsequent feelings of guilt may be at the root of a Christian's depression. Consulting with a trusted counselor often helps victims of depression or burnout define root causes, make necessary changes in their lives, and then move toward recovery.

But doubt, discouragement, and depression are also primary weapons used by Satan in the battle against our minds. He maligns God's character and faithfulness, redirects our focus on our problem instead of God's promise, and stimulates myopic spiritual vision in our hearts. In addition to dealing with other causes, exercising our spiritual muscles is also crucial in overcoming depression.

VICTORY IN THE SPIRITUAL REALM

James O. Fraser faced such a battle in 1913. He had labored for five years to establish Christian faith among the Lisu tribe in southwest China, with little success. Feeling suicidal, Fraser finally realized the "powers of darkness" were trying to get rid of him.

Just then—as the rainy season was at its dreariest—a magazine came in the mail. As Fraser read about Christ's triumph over Satan (based on Colossians 2:15), his faith began to rise. He felt he heard the Lord say, " ... Overcome, overcome, even as I also overcame." Fraser wrote to his prayer supporters:

"... Resist the devil" is also Scripture (James 4:7). And I found it worked! That cloud of depression dispersed. I found that I *could* have victory in the spiritual realm whenever I wanted it. The Lord Himself resisted the devil vocally: "Get thee behind me, Satan!" I, in humble dependence on Him, did the same. I talked to Satan at that time, using the promises of Scripture as weapons. And they worked. Right then, the terrible oppression began to pass away. One had to learn, gradually, how to use the new-found weapon of resistance.[2]

Spiritual warriors can learn a valuable lesson from the victory which followed. After he had learned to resist the enemy, Fraser worked successfully for thirty years among the Lisu and saw thousands turn to Christ. The Holy Spirit can help us in the same way: to recognize the source of the attack, obtain the help of a counselor if need be, and use the weapon of God's Word to overcome the enemy. The Word not only puts Satan to flight but also brings healing to our troubled souls.

SCRIPTURES

The LORD is my strength and my shield;
  my heart trusts in him, and I am helped.
My heart leaps for joy
  and I will give thanks to him in song.   **Psalm 28:7**

"For I know the plans I have for you," declares the LORD, "plans to prosper you and not to harm you, plans to give you hope and a future.   **Jeremiah 29:11**

... with us is the LORD our God to help us and to fight our battles....   **2 Chronicles 32:8**

Yet this I call to mind
    and therefore I have hope:
Because of the LORD's great love we are not consumed,
    for his compassions never fail.
They are new every morning;
    great is your faithfulness.
I say to myself, "The LORD is my portion;
    therefore I will wait for him."
The LORD is good to those whose hope is in him,
    to the one who seeks him;
it is good to wait quietly
    for the salvation of the LORD. **Lamentations 3:21-26**

You have made known to me the path of life;
    you will fill me with joy in your presence,
with eternal pleasures at your right hand. **Psalm 16:11**

... he restores my soul.
He guides me in paths of righteousness
    for his name's sake. **Psalm 23:3**

I will be glad and rejoice in your love,
    for you saw my affliction
and knew the anguish of my soul. **Psalm 31:7**

The righteous cry out, and the LORD hears them;
    he delivers them from all their troubles.
The LORD is close to the brokenhearted
    and saves those who are crushed in spirit.
A righteous man may have many troubles,
    but the LORD delivers him from them all. **Psalm 34:17-19**

If the LORD delights in a man's way,
    he makes his steps firm;
Though he stumble, he will not fall,
    for the LORD upholds him with his hand. **Psalm 37:23-24**

Why are you downcast, O my soul?
   Why so disturbed within me?
Put your hope in God,
   for I will yet praise him,
   my Savior and my God....

By day the LORD directs his love,
   at night his song is with me—
   a prayer to the God of my life.   **Psalm 42:5-6, 8**

Restore to me the joy of your salvation
   and grant me a willing spirit, to sustain me.   **Psalm 51:12**

Cast your cares on the LORD
   and he will sustain you;
   he will never let the righteous fall.   **Psalm 55:22**

Hear my cry, O God;
   listen to my prayer.
From the ends of the earth I call to you,
   I call as my heart grows faint;
   lead me to the rock that is higher than I.
For you have been my refuge,
   a strong tower against the foe.
I long to dwell in your tent forever
   and take refuge in the shelter of your wings.   **Psalm 61:1-4**

On my bed I remember you;
   I think of you through the watches of the night.
Because you are my help,
   I sing in the shadow of your wings.
My soul clings to you;
   your right hand upholds me.   **Psalm 63:6-8**

Come, let us sing for joy to the LORD;
   let us shout aloud to the Rock of our salvation.   **Psalm 95:1**

Praise the LORD, O my soul;
    all my inmost being, praise his holy name.
Praise the LORD, O my soul,
    and forget not all his benefits—
who forgives all your sins
    and heals all your diseases,
who redeems your life from the pit
    and crowns you with love and compassion,
who satisfies your desires with good things
    so that your youth is renewed like the eagle's.   **Psalm 103:1-5**

Be at rest once more, O my soul,
    for the LORD has been good to you.
For you, O LORD, have delivered my soul from death,
    my eyes from tears,
my feet from stumbling,
    that I may walk before the LORD
in the land of the living. **Psalm 116:7-9**

Shouts of joy and victory
    resound in the tents of the righteous:
"The LORD's right hand has done mighty things!"...
This is the day the LORD has made;
    let us rejoice and be glad in it. **Psalm 118:15, 24**

I wait for the LORD, my soul waits,
    and in his word I put my hope.
My soul waits for the Lord
    more than watchmen wait for the morning,...
put your hope in the LORD,
    for with the LORD is unfailing love
and with him is full redemption. **Psalm 130:5-7**

With joy you will draw water
    from the wells of salvation. **Isaiah 12:3**

You will keep in perfect peace
    him whose mind is steadfast,
because he trusts in you. **Isaiah 26:3**

I delight greatly in the LORD;
   my soul rejoices in my God.
For he has clothed me with garments of salvation
   and arrayed me in a robe of righteousness....   **Isaiah 61:10**

The LORD your God is with you,
   he is mighty to save.
He will take great delight in you,
   he will quiet you with his love,
he will rejoice over you with singing.   **Zephaniah 3:17**

"Come to me, all you who are weary and burdened, and I will
give you rest. Take my yoke upon you and learn from me, for
I am gentle and humble in heart, and you will find rest for
your souls. For my yoke is easy and my burden is light."
                                                    Matthew 11:28-30

"Peace I leave with you; my peace I give you. I do not give to
you as the world gives. Do not let your hearts be troubled and
do not be afraid." **John 14:27**

"If you obey my commands, you will remain in my love, just as
I have obeyed my Father's commands and remain in his love.
I have told you this so that my joy may be in you and that your
joy may be complete." **John 15:10-11**

... the disciples were filled with joy and with the Holy Spirit.
                                                    Acts 13:52

[God] gives life to the dead and calls things that are not as
though they were.
   Against all hope, Abraham in hope believed and so became
the father of many nations, just as it had been said to him....
                                                    Romans 4:17b-18a

And we know that in all things God works for the good of
those who love him, who have been called according to his
purpose.... If God is for us, who can be against us?
                                                    Romans 8:28, 31

For the kingdom of God is not a matter of eating and drinking, but of righteousness, peace and joy in the Holy Spirit....

Romans 14:17

May the God of hope fill you with all joy and peace as you trust in him, so that you may overflow with hope by the power of the Holy Spirit. **Romans 15:13**

Therefore we do not lose heart. Though outwardly we are wasting away, yet inwardly we are being renewed day by day. For our light and momentary troubles are achieving for us an eternal glory that far outweighs them all. So we fix our eyes not on what is seen, but on what is unseen. For what is seen is temporary, but what is unseen is eternal. **2 Corinthians 4:16-18**

Do not be anxious about anything, but in everything, by prayer and petition, with thanksgiving, present your requests to God. And the peace of God, which transcends all understanding, will guard your hearts and your minds in Christ Jesus.

Finally, brothers, whatever is true, whatever is noble, whatever is right, whatever is pure, whatever is lovely, whatever is admirable—if anything is excellent or praiseworthy—think about such things. Whatever you have learned or received or heard from me, or seen in me—put it into practice. And the God of peace will be with you. **Philippians 4:6-9**

Since, then, you have been raised with Christ, set your hearts on things above, where Christ is seated at the right hand of God. Set your minds on things above, not on earthly things.

Colossians 3:1-2

Let us fix our eyes on Jesus, the author and perfecter of our faith, who for the joy set before him endured the cross, scorning its shame, and sat down at the right hand of the throne of God. **Hebrews 12:2**

... prepare your minds for action; be self-controlled; set your hope fully on the grace to be given you when Jesus Christ is revealed. As obedient children, do not conform to the evil desires you had when you lived in ignorance.   1 Peter 1:13-14

Humble yourselves, therefore, under God's mighty hand, that he may lift you up in due time. Cast all your anxiety on him because he cares for you.   1 Peter 5:6-7

PRAYER

Lord, thank you that I don't have to live under a cloud of depression. I praise you that you are at work even now, restoring the joy of my salvation, and restoring my soul in every area. Father, help me to put on a garment of praise instead of a spirit of heaviness. Help me to fix my eyes upon Jesus, and not upon my problems. May I find my comfort in you. Amen.

11

Freedom from Anxiety and Fear

FEAR... FRIGHT... DREAD... PANIC. All these words come from the same root word. Many of those who inhabit today's world seem plagued by fear. We fear the future, failure, financial loss. We fear being rejected, disapproved, left out, unloved, or ignored. We fear disease and death. We fear life itself.

Jesus came to conquer all those fears: "... he too shared in their humanity so that by his death he might destroy him who holds the power of death—that is, the devil—and free those who all their lives were held in slavery by their fear of death (Hebrews 2:14-15).

When God raised Christ from the dead by the power of the Holy Spirit, he proved for time and eternity that Satan is defeated. That same Spirit abides in every one who believes in Jesus as savior. As Scripture says, "And if the Spirit of him who raised Jesus from the dead is living in you, he who raised

Christ from the dead will also give life to your mortal bodies through his Spirit, who lives in you" (Romans 8:11).

Knowing that the resurrected Christ dwells in us should eradicate any fear stirred up by the enemy. This contemporary song helps us keep the proper perspective:

Every Morning Is Easter Morning *

Ev'ry morning is Easter Morning from now on!
Ev'ry day's Resurrection Day, the past is over and gone!
Goodbye guilt, goodbye fear, good riddance!
    Hello Lord, hello sun!
I am one of the Easter People! My new life has begun!

Ev'ry morning is Easter Morning from now on!
Ev'ry day's Resurrection Day, the past is over and gone!
Daily news is so bad it seems the Good News seldom gets
    heard.
Get it straight from the Easter People: God's in charge!
    Spread the word!

FEAR VS. TRUST

Pastor D. James Kennedy shares a story from the life of Abraham Lincoln that illustrates the futility of fear:

[Lincoln] told of the days when he was a circuit-riding lawyer. He would travel to all the small towns throughout the region, wherever court was being held. This of course involved frequent river crossings, particularly of the notorious Fox River, turbulent and very dangerous in times of heavy rain.

On one occasion, after crossing several rivers with no small amount of difficulty, Lincoln's companion shook his head and said, "If these rivers are this bad, whatever will it be like when we must cross the Fox?" As it happened, that night they met an itinerant Methodist minister at the inn where they were staying. They asked if he knew the Fox River. "Oh, yes," the preacher said. "I know it well. I have crossed it innumerable times these many long years." They asked if he had any advice about how they might cross it safely.

"Absolutely!" he grinned. "I have discovered a secret about crossing the Fox River which I never fail to keep in mind. It is this: I never cross the Fox River until I *reach* the Fox River. Good night, gentlemen."[1]

Most of the things we fear either never happen or turn out not to be so fearsome after all—a lesson the Methodist minister obviously had learned. Scripture says repeatedly, "Do not be afraid...." David's words can become a prayer for us when we feel the threat of fear:

> When I am afraid,
>   I will trust in you.
> In God, whose word I praise,
>   in God I trust; I will not be afraid.
> What can mortal man do to me? **Psalm 56:3-4**

ROLE MODELS IN THE BIBLE

Joshua and Caleb demonstrate a stirring triumph of faith over fear. After God told the Israelites to possess the land across the river Jordan, these two scouts were among those sent by Moses to explore Canaan. All twelve spies agreed it was a wonderful land, just as God had promised. But ten of the spies were ruled by fear: "We can't attack those people; they are stronger than we are.... We seemed like grasshoppers in our own eyes, and we looked the same to them" (Numbers 13:31, 33).

Standing against the majority, Joshua and Caleb exhorted the people to stand on faith in God's promise: "... do not rebel against the Lord. And do not be afraid of the people of the land, because we will swallow them up. Their protection is gone, but the LORD is with us. Do not be afraid of them" (Numbers 14:9).

The Israelites listened to the fearful spies and ignored the appeal of Joshua and Caleb. As a consequence, they spent forty more years wandering in the wilderness. Nonetheless, God honored the faith of these two spiritual warriors. When the Israelites did cross over into Canaan, Joshua led them in battle. And God said of Caleb: "But because my servant Caleb has a different spirit and follows me wholeheartedly, I will bring him into the land he went to, and his descendants will inherit it" (Numbers 14:24). God rewards those who faithfully stand on his promises.

Nehemiah offers another example of how to handle fear. As he was directing the rebuilding of the walls of Jerusalem, his enemies ridiculed and threatened him. Nehemiah responded by assigning half the workers to continue building with their swords at their sides, and the other half to stand guard over them with additional weapons: "... I stood up and said to the nobles, the officials and the rest of the people, 'don't be afraid of them. Remember the Lord, who is great and awesome, and fight for your brothers, your sons and your daughters, your wives and your homes.... Wherever you hear the sound of the trumpet, join us there. Our God will fight for us!'" (Nehemiah 4:14, 20).

The enemy *repeatedly* tried to instill fear in the people and to lure Nehemiah to come down off the wall and talk things over. Nehemiah refused. Later he wrote: "They were all trying to frighten us, thinking, 'Their hands will get too weak for the work, and it will not be completed.' But I prayed, 'Now strengthen my hands'" (Nehemiah 6:9).

And God did. They finished the work in record time—an example of aggressive faith winning the battle over crippling fear.

In our moments of fear, we too can declare what God's Word says—even quoting it aloud—and remind the devil that our God will surely fight for us.

SCRIPTURES

Do not be afraid of them; the LORD your God himself will fight for you.... But do not be afraid of them; remember well what the LORD your God did to Pharaoh and to all Egypt.

Deuteronomy 3:22; 7:18

When you go to war against your enemies and see horses and chariots and an army greater than yours, do not be afraid of them, because the LORD your God, who brought you up out of Egypt, will be with you. *Deuteronomy 20:1*

Be strong and courageous. Do not be afraid or terrified because of them, for the LORD your God goes with you.... The LORD himself goes before you and will be with you; he will never leave you nor forsake you. Do not be afraid; do not be discouraged. *Deuteronomy 31:6, 8*

... This is what the LORD says to you: "Do not be afraid or discouraged because of this vast army. For the battle is not yours, but God's."...

The fear of God came upon all the kingdoms of the countries when they heard how the LORD had fought against the enemies of Israel. And the kingdom of Jehoshaphat was at peace, for his God had given him rest on every side.

2 Chronicles 20:15, 29-30

You will be protected from the lash of the tongue,
and need not fear when destruction comes.
You will laugh at destruction and famine,
and need not fear the beasts of the earth. *Job 5:21-22*

But you are a shield around me, O LORD;
you bestow glory on me and lift up my head....

I will not fear the tens of thousands
    drawn up against me on every side.   **Psalm 3:3, 6**

Even though I walk
    through the valley of the shadow of death,
I will fear no evil,
    for you are with me;
your rod and your staff,
    they comfort me.   **Psalm 23:4**

The LORD is my light and my salvation—
    whom shall I fear?
The LORD is the stronghold of my life—
    of whom shall I be afraid?
When evil men advance against me
  to devour my flesh,
when my enemies and my foes attack me,
    they will stumble and fall.
Though an army besiege me,
    my heart will not fear;
though war break out against me,
    even then will I be confident.   **Psalm 27:1-3**

God is our refuge and strength,
    an ever-present help in trouble.
Therefore we will not fear,
    though the earth give way
and the mountains fall into the heart of the sea,
    though its waters roar and foam
and the mountains quake with their surging.   **Psalm 46:1-3**

Praise the LORD.
Blessed is the man who fears the LORD,
    who finds great delight in his commands....
He will have no fear of bad news;
    his heart is steadfast, trusting in the LORD.

His heart is secure, he will have no fear;
    in the end he will look in triumph on his foes.   **Psalm 112:1, 7-8**

... when you lie down, you will not be afraid;
    when you lie down, your sleep will be sweet.
Have no fear of sudden disaster
    or of the ruin that overtakes the wicked,
for the LORD will be your confidence
    and will keep your foot from being snared.   **Proverbs 3:24-26**

... he will delight in the fear of the LORD.
He will not judge by what he sees with his eyes,
    or decide by what he hears with his ears....   **Isaiah 11:3**

You will keep in perfect peace
    him whose mind is steadfast,
because he trusts in you.   **Isaiah 26:3**

So this is what the Sovereign LORD says:
"See, I lay a stone in Zion,
    a tested stone,
a precious cornerstone for a sure foundation;
    the one who trusts will never be dismayed."   **Isaiah 28:16**

So do not fear, for I am with you;
    do not be dismayed, for I am your God.
I will strengthen you and help you;
    I will uphold you with my righteous right hand....
But now, this is what the LORD says—
    he who created you, O Jacob,
    he who formed you, O Israel:
"Fear not, for I have redeemed you;
I have summoned you by name; you are mine."   **Isaiah 41:10; 43:1**

"... I am the first and I am the last;
    apart from me there is no God....
Do not tremble, do not be afraid.

Did I not proclaim this and foretell it long ago?
You are my witnesses. Is there any God besides me?
   No, there is no other Rock; I know not one." **Isaiah 44:6, 8**

In righteousness you will be established:
Tyranny will be far from you;
   you will have nothing to fear.
Terror will be far removed;
   it will not come near you. **Isaiah 54:14**

This is what the LORD says:
   "Do not learn the ways of the nations
      or be terrified by signs in the sky,
    though the nations are terrified by them....
   Like a scarecrow in a melon patch,
      their idols cannot speak;
   they must be carried
      because they cannot walk.
   Do not fear them;
      they can do no harm
      nor can they do any good." **Jeremiah 10:2, 5**

" ... blessed is the man who trusts in the LORD,
   whose confidence is in him.
He will be like a tree planted by the water
   that sends out its roots by the stream.
It does not fear when heat comes;
   its leaves are always green.
It has no worries in a year of drought
   and never fails to bear fruit." **Jeremiah 17:7-8**

Do not be afraid of the king of Babylon, whom you now fear.
Do not be afraid of him, declares the LORD, for I am with you
and will save you and deliver you from his hands. **Jeremiah 42:11**

"Do not be afraid of those who kill the body but cannot kill
the soul. Rather, be afraid of the One who can destroy both
soul and body in hell." **Matthew 10:28**

"Do not be afraid, little flock, for your Father has been pleased to give you the kingdom". Luke 12:32

"Peace I leave with you; my peace I give you. I do not give to you as the world gives. Do not let your hearts be troubled and do not be afraid." John 14:27

"I have told you these things, so that in me you may have peace. In this world you will have trouble. But take heart! I have overcome the world." John 16:33

For you did not receive a spirit that makes you a slave again to fear, but you received the Spirit of sonship. And by him we cry, "Abba, Father." Romans 8:15

... If God is for us, who can be against us?... For I am convinced that neither death nor life, neither angels nor demons, neither the present nor the future, nor any powers, neither height nor depth, nor anything else in all creation, will be able to separate us from the love of God that is in Christ Jesus our Lord. Romans 8:31, 38-39

... we were harassed at every turn—conflicts on the outside, fears within. But God, who comforts the downcast, comforted us by the coming of Titus, and... also by the comfort you had given him. 2 Corinthians 7:5-7

For God did not give us a spirit of timidity, but a spirit of power, of love and of self-discipline. 2 Timothy 1:7

... we say with confidence,
"The Lord is my helper; I will not be afraid.
What can man do to me?" Hebrews 13:6

But even if you should suffer for what is right, you are blessed. "Do not fear what they fear; do not be frightened." But in your hearts set apart Christ as Lord. Always be prepared to

give an answer to everyone who asks you to give the reason for
the hope that you have.... 1 Peter 3:14-15

There is no fear in love. But perfect love drives out fear,
because fear has to do with punishment. The one who fears is
not made perfect in love. 1 John 4:18

PRAYER AGAINST FEAR

Father, at those times when I am afraid, let me throw myself
upon your mercy. Give me the confidence of the Shepherd,
who could say he feared no evil. Help me always to remember
that the fact of the Resurrection destroys the enemy's power
to make me afraid. Thank you that your perfect love casts out
all my fears. I put my trust in you. Amen.

12

Freedom from Guilt

My guilt has overwhelmed me
　like a burden too heavy to bear....
You know my folly, O God;
　my guilt is not hidden from you. **Psalms 38:4; 69:5**

T HESE WORDS OF THE PSALMIST strike a familiar note. We have all experienced remorse over wrong words and wrong actions, or regret because we failed to speak or act when we should have done so.

We can't go back and do it over, but we can't seem to shake the guilt. The heavy baggage of our past prevents our moving ahead into the future. Like Adam and Eve, we want to hide from God. Seeking to dull the pain of guilt, many find themselves trapped in destructive addictions.

God knows all about guilt. His antidote is grace, God's unmerited favor. We actually deserve punishment for our sins, but God sent Jesus into the world to bear the punishment for every sinful person who's ever lived. Accepting his gift of grace releases us from the prison of guilt.

In Old Testament times, when a person broke the law and offended God, he brought a lamb as a "guilt offering." The priest offered it as a sacrifice to atone for the sin. Long before Christ's birth, Isaiah prophesied that the Messiah himself would become a guilt offering:

We all, like sheep, have gone astray,
    each of us has turned to his own way;
and the LORD has laid on him
    the iniquity of us all....
Yet was the LORD's will to crush him and cause him
        to suffer,
    and though the LORD makes his life a guilt offering,
he will see his offspring and prolong his days,
    and the will of the LORD will prosper in his hand.
                                                    Isaiah 53:6, 10

When the Holy Spirit convicts us of sin, it is our place to confess it, to turn from it, and to receive God's forgiveness and cleansing. "If we confess our sins, he is faithful and just and will forgive us our sins and purify us from all unrighteousness" (1 John 1:9). John goes on to proclaim Jesus as the sacrificial lamb for all: "... But if anybody does sin, we have one who speaks to the Father in our defense—Jesus Christ, the Righteous One. He is the atoning sacrifice for our sins, and not only for ours but also for the sins of the whole world" (1 John 2:1-2).

To be effective in spiritual warfare, it is crucial that we distinguish between true guilt and false guilt. The devil will try every way possible to keep us carrying a load of guilt— whether true or false. Dr. Diane Langberg, a clinical psychologist, discusses this common dilemma:

True guilt is, of course, that which results from God's judgment, not man's. It is not myself or another who can determine my guilt, but God himself.... If the only just judge is God, then I must go to him to decide whether or not I am guilty.

... There is no simple formula for living a guilt-free life. Nor is there an easy answer for how to determine the validity of the guilt we feel. It involves constantly going back to God and looking at our lives, asking him to sharpen our insights so that we see ourselves more and more clearly.[1]

False guilt is what you feel when you assume the blame for someone else's wrongdoing. Feeling sure they must have done something wrong to deserve it, abuse victims often carry such a burden. But when a victim finally learns to release the burden of false guilt and to repent for his or her own sin of unforgiveness in the matter, the bondage is broken. In some cases, abuse victims may need the help of a counselor to work through the feelings of guilt and anger until they are able to forgive their abusers and find freedom.

If the devil keeps stirring up guilt—even after you've confessed and repented before the Lord and received his cleansing—you need to vigorously stand against the adversary. You can simply say, "Yes, I did that and it was wrong, but I've asked my Heavenly Father to forgive me. Satan, you cannot keep tormenting my mind with that offense. The blood of Jesus covers it. You be gone, in Jesus' name."

Ed Cole makes this observation about guilt and forgiveness: "Every man must answer for his own actions. And he must answer to God alone. That is why Calvary, where Christ died, is so important. It is the only place in the world where sin can be placed and forgiveness from God received. The only place where guilt can be released."[2]

SCRIPTURES ABOUT CONFESSING GUILT

David was conscience-stricken after he had counted the fighting men, and he said to the LORD, "I have sinned greatly in what I have done. Now, O LORD, I beg you, take away the guilt of your servant. I have done a very foolish thing." **2 Samuel 24:10**

... [I] fell on my knees with my hands spread out to the LORD my God and prayed:
>"O my God, I am too ashamed and disgraced to lift up my face to you, my God, because our sins are higher than our heads and our guilt has reached to the heavens...."
Ezra 9:5-6

Against you, you only, have I sinned
 and done what is evil in your sight,
so that you are proved right when you speak
 and justified when you judge....
Hide your face from my sins
 and blot out all my iniquity. **Psalm 51:4, 9**

O LORD, we acknowledge our wickedness
 and the guilt of our fathers;
we have indeed sinned against you. **Jeremiah 14:20**

I said, "O LORD, have mercy on me;
 heal me, for I have sinned against you." **Psalm 41:4**

We have sinned, even as our fathers did;
 we have done wrong and acted wickedly. **Psalm 106:6**

If we claim we have not sinned, we make him out to be a liar and his word has no place in our lives. **1 John 1:10**

SCRIPTURES ABOUT REMOVING GUILT

Then I acknowledged my sin to you
 and did not cover up my iniquity.
I said, "I will confess
 my transgressions to the LORD"—

and you forgave
  the guilt of my sin. **Psalm 32:5**

"When [the Counselor] comes, he will convict the world of guilt in regard to sin and righteousness and judgment."

John 16:8

... let us draw near to God with a sincere heart in full assurance of faith, having our hearts sprinkled to cleanse us from a guilty conscience and having our bodies washed with pure water. **Hebrews 10:22**

"Woe to me!" I cried. "I am ruined! For I am a man of unclean lips, and I live among a people of unclean lips, and my eyes have seen the King, the Lord Almighty."
  Then one of the seraphs flew to me with a live coal in his hand, which he had taken with tongs from the altar. With it he touched my mouth and said, "See, this has touched your lips; your guilt is taken away and your sin atoned for." **Isaiah 6:5-7**

... then hear from heaven, your dwelling place. Forgive and act; deal with each man according to all he does, since you know his heart (for you alone know the hearts of all men)....

1 Kings 8:39

  "Forgive us our debts,
    as we also have forgiven our debtors...."
  "For if you forgive men when they sin against you, your heavenly Father will also forgive you. But if you do not forgive men their sins, your Father will not forgive your sins."

Matthew 6:12, 14-15

"And when you stand praying, if you hold anything against anyone, forgive him, so that your Father in heaven may forgive you your sins." **Mark 11:25**

Bear with each other and forgive whatever grievances you may have against one another. Forgive as the Lord forgave you.

Colossians 3:13

It is for freedom that Christ has set us free. Stand firm, then, and do not let yourselves be burdened again by a yoke of slavery....

You, my brothers, were called to be free. But do not use your freedom to indulge the sinful nature; rather, serve one another in love. Galatians 5:1, 13

PRAYER

Thank you, Jesus, for coming to earth to die as a sin offering for me. Thank you that whenever I sin and am burdened by guilt, I need only come to you with true repentance and you wipe my sin-slate clean. I am cleansed by your precious shed blood. Restored to fellowship with the Father.

What an exchange. What a release. What a gift! Praise you, Lord. Help me to continue to walk in your freedom, and to help set other captives free. In Jesus' name, Amen.

13

Overcoming Grief and Disappointment

G RIEF IS USUALLY ASSOCIATED with the loss of a loved one through death—probably the most traumatic grief experience any of us encounters in life. But we also experience grief and disappointment due to other losses: losing a spouse through divorce, losing friends through broken relationships, losing companionship when friends or children move away, losing a job, losing one's home or valuable possessions, losing one's first love, losing one's hope of achieving a goal.

Any sort of significant loss can throw us into emotional turmoil. Counselor Alfred Ells describes grief as "the natural, unavoidable emotional reaction to loss, a process we emotionally work through until we arrive at a place of acceptance, a place that says, 'I lost and it is okay.'"[1] Working through this reaction inevitably leaves us vulnerable to the attack of the evil one. We need to keep our spiritual radar especially alert during such periods in our lives.

As a process of healing, grieving should follow a natural course over a span of time. Secular counselors say that process can last from one to three years or longer, depending on the severity of the loss. A premature death or a death by suicide or murder is much more traumatic and usually requires even more time to process.

Be aware that unresolved, prolonged grief opens the door to spiritual, physical, and emotional problems that can eventually paralyze a person's spiritual progress. To recover, the Christian must go through the same stages of grief as anyone else. However, we might find the process accelerated the more we make use of our spiritual resources. The lows don't have to be as low as for those who grieve with no hope (see 1 Thessalonians 4:13).

Christian counselor H. Dale Wright defines four tasks of grief:

1. Acceptance rather than denial. Face the reality of what has happened, even though it opens a floodgate of pain.
2. Allow yourself to feel the pain rather than ignoring or repressing it. Stifled emotional pain shows up in varied ways—such as physical ailments, addictive behavior, or irrational anger—and greatly hinders the healing process. Talk about the loss; allow expression of your emotions.
3. Adjust to an environment where that person (or place, job, etc.) is missing. Reorganize your life accordingly. Avoid indulging in self-pity or isolating yourself either physically or emotionally from other believers.
4. Withdraw the emotional energy invested in that person, place or job, and reinvest it in someone or something else. Begin to live life for the present and the future, not in the past.[2]

Christians can suffer severe frustration in their walk with the Lord because they have never properly grieved past losses.

Abuse victims, in particular, need to mourn their loss of the innocence of childhood. This time of grieving need not be lengthy, but the loss and sense of betrayal should be acknowledged so that healing can occur.

If you recognize yourself in this scenario, be aware that Satan wants to keep you in a state of spiritual limbo. You can overcome the enemy by asking the Holy Spirit to reveal to you any such unresolved grief, lead you on to healing, and then empower you to minister to others with the same needs. Alfred Ells wisely says:

> If we embrace our loss and work through the grief with Jesus, we will come to acceptance and resolution.... Each loss we suffer is an opportunity to invite Jesus deeper into our lives by making him our security instead of what we lost.
>
> ... When I finally cried my tears of loss and profoundly shared with Jesus my anger, fear, and guilt, I felt his acceptance. At first it felt strange to mourn something that had happened more than twenty years ago. But it worked. I felt the self-judgment, fear, and shame dissipate.[3]

Our Lord Jesus knew what it was like to be sorrowful and troubled. When his friend Lazarus died, Jesus wept. He wept over the city of Jerusalem. On a dark night in Gethsemane before his arrest and crucifixion, he asked three close friends to keep watch with him because his soul was "... overwhelmed with sorrow to the point of death" (Matthew 26:38). Because Jesus knew sorrow in his own personal life, he identifies with us in our grief. And when we allow him to, he can help us walk through it in victory. Scripture also offers many words of comfort and healing for the believer who is working through grief and disappointment.

SCRIPTURES

I am worn out from groaning;
 all night long I flood my bed with weeping

and drench my couch with tears....
The LORD has heard my cry for mercy;
    the LORD accepts my prayer. **Psalm 6:6, 9**

Have no fear of sudden disaster
    or of the ruin that overtakes the wicked,
for the LORD will be your confidence
    and will keep your foot from being snared. **Proverbs 3:25-26**

God is our refuge and strength,
    an ever-present help in trouble. **Psalm 46:1**

From the ends of the earth I call to you,
    I call as my heart grows faint;
lead me to the rock that is higher than I. **Psalm 61:2**

Find rest, O my soul, in God alone;
    my hope comes from him.
He alone is my rock and my salvation;
    he is my fortress, I will not be shaken....
Trust in him at all times, O people;
    pour out your hearts to him, for God is our refuge.
                           Psalm 62:5-6, 8

The lowly he sets on high,
    and those who mourn are lifted to safety. **Job 5:11**

... a time to weep and a time to laugh,
    a time to mourn and a time to dance... **Ecclesiastes 3:4**

But you, O God, do see trouble and grief;
    you consider it to take it in hand.
The victim commits himself to you;
    you are the helper of the fatherless. **Psalm 10:14**

Even though I walk
    through the valley of the shadow of death,
I will fear no evil,

for you are with me;
your rod and your staff,
    they comfort me. **Psalm 23:4**

Be merciful to me, O LORD, for I am in distress;
    my eyes grow weak with sorrow,
my soul and my body with grief. **Psalm 31:9**

For he does not willingly bring affliction
    or grief to the children of men. **Lamentations 3:33**

My comfort in my suffering is this:
Your promise preserves my life....
May your unfailing love be my comfort,
    according to your promise to your servant. **Psalm 119:50, 76**

With joy you will draw water
    from the wells of salvation. **Isaiah 12:3**

I will go before you
    and will level the mountains;
I will break down gates of bronze
    and cut through bars of iron.
I will give you the treasures of darkness,
    riches stored in secret places,
so that you may know that I am the LORD,
    the God of Israel, who summons you by name. **Isaiah 45:2-3**

The Spirit of the Sovereign LORD is on me,...
    [to] provide for those who grieve in Zion—
to bestow on them a crown of beauty instead of ashes,
the oil of gladness
    instead of mourning,
and a garment of praise
    instead of a spirit of despair.
They will be called oaks of righteousness,

a planting of the LORD
for the display of his splendor.   Isaiah 61:1, 3

Then maidens will dance and be glad,
   young men and old as well.
I will turn their mourning into gladness;
   I will give them comfort and joy instead of sorrow.
                                                      Jeremiah 31:13

Praise be to the God and Father of our Lord Jesus Christ, the
Father of compassion and the God of all comfort, who comforts us in all our troubles, so that we can comfort those in any
trouble with the comfort we ourselves have received from
God. For just as the sufferings of Christ flow over into our
lives, so also through Christ our comfort overflows.... And our
hope for you is firm, because we know that just as you share in
our sufferings, so also you share in our comfort.
                                                      2 Corinthians 1:3-5, 7

But the fruit of the Spirit is love, joy, peace, patience, kindness, goodness, faithfulness...   Galatians 5:22

... one thing I do: Forgetting what is behind and straining
toward what is ahead, I press on toward the goal to win the
prize for which God has called me heavenward in Christ Jesus.
                                                      Philippians 3:13-14

Brothers, we do not want you to be ignorant about those who
fall asleep, or to grieve like the rest of men, who have no hope.
We believe that Jesus died and rose again and so we believe
that God will bring with Jesus those who have fallen asleep in
him.... For the Lord himself will come down from heaven,
with a loud command, with the voice of the archangel and
with the trumpet call of God, and the dead in Christ will rise
first.   1 Thessalonians 4:13-14, 16

Let us fix our eyes on Jesus, the author and perfecter of our
faith, who for the joy set before him endured the cross, scorn-

ing its shame, and sat down at the right hand of the throne of God. **Hebrews 12:2**

Consider it pure joy, my brothers, whenever you face trials of many kinds.... **James 1:2**

In this you greatly rejoice, though now for a little while you may have had to suffer grief in all kinds of trials....

But you are a chosen people, a royal priesthood, a holy nation, a people belonging to God, that you may declare the praises of him who called you out of darkness into his wonderful light....

But rejoice that you participate in the sufferings of Christ, so that you may be overjoyed when his glory is revealed.

1 Peter 1:6; 2:9; 4:13

For the Lamb at the center of the throne will be their shepherd;

he will lead them to springs of living water.

And God will wipe away every tear from their eyes....

... There will be no more death or mourning or crying or pain, for the old order of things has passed away.

Revelation 7:17; 21:4

PRAYER FOR THE GRIEVING

Father, I acknowledge to you my pain, my anger, my fear, my sadness, and sense of feeling overwhelmed. Lord, I take refuge in you because you are the Rock that is higher than I. I place myself in your hands to be led through this process of grief and sorrow, knowing that you will take me at my own pace.

Father, I trust in you for total restoration of body, soul, and spirit. Thank you for being my confidence, firm and strong, and for keeping my foot from being caught in hidden pitfalls of the enemy. I choose to put my trust in you, even though I don't always understand. Hover over me with the comfort of your Holy Spirit, in Jesus' name. Amen.

PRAYER FOR THE DISAPPOINTED

Father, this disappointment is almost more than I can bear. You said that the Holy Spirit would comfort us. You said others would comfort us. I need the assurance of that comfort. Thank you that you know the road ahead of me and ordain my steps. Help me to trust you in these uncertain times and to walk in the confidence of your love for me. Lord, help me to focus on you, instead of on my own hurt.

I refuse to allow the enemy to steal my joy. Lord, my joy is in you, and does not depend upon favorable circumstances. Thank you that you alone are my source of life. Thank you for dying for every hurt I will ever need to endure. I rejoice in you today. Amen.

14

Regaining Self-Esteem

O LORD, you have searched me
and you know me.
You know when I sit and when I rise;
you perceive my thoughts from afar.
You discern my going out and my lying down;
you are familiar with all my ways....

For you created my inmost being;
you knit me together in my mother's womb.
I praise you because I am fearfully and wonderfully
made;
your works are wonderful,
I know that full well. **Psalm 139:1-3, 13-14**

T HIS PSALM ASSURES US that God knew about each one of us
even before our conception. Though we are made in the
image of the Creator God, joint heirs with Christ, many believers continue to suffer from low self-esteem, insecurity, and

anxiety. Why? Mostly because we lose sight of what a holy heritage we have!

Often a person's low self-esteem stems from a background of physical, emotional, or sexual abuse, in which case professional counseling may be necessary. God's desire is that you see yourself as his beloved child. Dr. Diane Langberg, a clinical psychologist, says:

> We may feel useless and inconsequential, of no value to God or others, but how God views us does not depend on how we view ourselves with our own eyes.
>
> ... We have a wrong view of ourselves. Rather than keeping God central, man has put himself in the center.[1]

Dr. Langberg points out how some people invest a great deal of energy in hating themselves, continually focusing on how bad, unimportant, and worthless they are. The enemy knows our every weakness and loves to constantly toss in his two cents, or more often his silver dollars. The accuser is ever at hand reminding us of how low we can stoop.

Yet when God sent his Son to die for us, he graphically demonstrated how highly he values us. By sending the Holy Spirit to dwell in our hearts, God again intervened to make us look like our heavenly Father. Paul describes this process of transformation: "And we who with unveiled faces all reflect the Lord's glory, are being transformed into his likeness with ever-increasing glory, which comes from the Lord, who is the Spirit" (2 Corinthians 3:18).

We need to remember that being transformed into God's likeness requires time, just as growing fruit requires time. As a matter of fact, we will not be ripe for the picking until we draw our last breath on this earth. Our encouragement must come from seeing even the smallest steps of growth along the way.

People who suffer low self-esteem are sometimes consumed with anxiety—varying from mild concern to paralyzing dread, or from nagging doubts to excessive brooding. Satan's secret ploy is to assault our minds and emotions, planting thoughts that don't line up with God's truth, and keeping us focused on our own needs. The mind often proves to be our biggest battleground.

Scripture exhorts us to reject these wrong thoughts and to meditate on God's truth. But we must personally choose to implement these remedies for anxiety. God never violates anyone's free will.

SCRIPTURES FOR REJECTING WRONG THOUGHTS

We demolish arguments and every pretension that sets itself up against the knowledge of God, and we take captive every thought to make it obedient to Christ. **2 Corinthians 10:5**

Search me, O God, and know my heart;
    test me and know my anxious thoughts.
See if there is any offensive way in me,
    and lead me in the way everlasting. **Psalm 139:23-24**

You will keep in perfect peace
    him whose mind is steadfast,
    because he trusts in you.
Trust in the LORD forever,
    for the LORD, the LORD, is the Rock eternal. **Isaiah 26:3-4**

Set a guard over my mouth, O LORD;
    keep watch over the door of my lips.
Let not my heart be drawn to what is evil,
    to take part in wicked deeds
with men who are evildoers.... **Psalm 141:3-4**

Do not conform any longer to the pattern of this world, but be transformed by the renewing of your mind. Then you will be able to test and approve what God's will is—his good, pleasing and perfect will. **Romans 12:2**

You were taught, with regard to your former way of life, to put off your old self, which is being corrupted by its deceitful desires; to be made new in the attitude of your minds; and to put on the new self, created to be like God in true righteousness and holiness. **Ephesians 4:22-24**

... I have often told you before and now say again even with tears, many live as enemies of the cross of Christ.... Their mind is on earthly things. But our citizenship is in heaven. And we eagerly await a Savior from there, the Lord Jesus Christ, who, by the power that enables him to bring everything under his control, will transform our lowly bodies so that they will be like his glorious body. **Philippians 3:18-21**

SCRIPTURES ON MEDITATING ON GOD'S WORD

Do not let this Book of the Law depart from your mouth; meditate on it day and night, so that you may be careful to do everything written in it. Then you will be prosperous and successful. **Joshua 1:8**

I will meditate on all your works
  and consider all your mighty deeds. **Psalm 77:12**

"And you, my son Solomon, acknowledge the God of your father, and serve him with wholehearted devotion and with a willing mind, for the LORD searches every heart and understands every motive behind the thoughts. If you seek him, he will be found by you; but if you forsake him, he will reject you forever." **1 Chronicles 28:9**

Jesus replied: "'Love the Lord your God with all your heart and with all your soul and with all your mind.' This is the first and greatest commandment...." **Matthew 22:37-38**

... But we have the mind of Christ. **1 Corinthians 2:16**

Therefore, if anyone is in Christ, he is a new creation; the old has gone, the new has come!   2 Corinthians 5:17

OTHER SCRIPTURES

My frame was not hidden from you
    when I was made in the secret place.
When I was woven together in the depths of the earth,
    your eyes saw my unformed body.
All the days ordained for me
    were written in your book
    before one of them came to be.
How precious to me are your thoughts, O God!
How vast is the sum of them!
Were I to count them,
    they would outnumber the grains of sand.
When I awake,
    I am still with you.   Psalm 139:15-18

The LORD will fulfill his purpose for me....   Psalm 138:8

The tongue has the power of life and death....   Proverbs 18:21

Many are the plans in a man's heart,
  but it is the LORD's purpose that prevails.   Proverbs 19:21

Then Job replied to the LORD:
"I know that you can do all things;
  no plan of yours can be thwarted."   Job 42:1-2

Forget the former things;
    do not dwell on the past.
See, I am doing a new thing!
Now it springs up; do you not perceive it?...   Isaiah 43:18-19

... If God is for us, who can be against us?   Romans 8:31

But because of his great love for us, God, who is rich in mercy, made us alive with Christ even when we were dead in transgressions.... And God raised us up with Christ and seated us with him in the heavenly realms in Christ Jesus.... **Ephesians 2:4-6**

For we are God's workmanship, created in Christ Jesus to do good works, which God prepared in advance for us to do.

Ephesians 2:10

... I [Paul] was shown mercy so that in me, the worst of sinners, Christ Jesus might display his unlimited patience as an example for those who would believe on him and receive eternal life. **1 Timothy 1:16**

... God is love. Whoever lives in love lives in God, and God in him. **1 John 4:16**

PRAYER

Lord, I am forever grateful that you lifted me out of despair and put my feet on solid ground. Thank you for loving me enough to die for me—even when I was unlovable. You know the plans you have for me; I don't have to worry and fret about them. Help me always to yield to your plan as you conform me to your own image. I know that if you are for me— and you are—then no plan of the enemy will succeed. Lord, I pray that others will see your beauty in me. Amen.

PART THREE

Fighting on the Homefront

15

Warfare for Your Marriage and Broken Relationships

PERHAPS YOU CONSIDER THAT YOUR marriage has been reasonably healthy most of the time over the years since your wedding. You and your spouse are both Christians, you're usually compatible, and you share fairly common goals. Yet you can see yourself in one or more of these scenarios. In fact, you may even be deeply concerned about how often you:

- Find yourself bickering with your mate over relatively minor matters, then holding a grudge afterwards.
- Feel resentment when your spouse spends money without first talking it over with you.
- Feel annoyed when your spouse suggests spending Christmas with a relative you don't like.
- Feel neglected when home alone while your spouse is at a meeting in which you are not included, or is spending

time with people you feel are a negative influence on him/her.

- Find yourself saying or hearing "why are you always late?" (or some other negative "always" or "never" expression).
- Feel resentment when your spouse is more polite or attentive to others (especially of the opposite sex) than to you.
- Find your spouse is sure to misunderstand if you try to express your true feelings—so you stifle them.
- Start measuring the time that has passed since the last compliment, "I love you" gift or romantic experience.
- Realize you've been comparing your companion unfavorably with a former sweetheart or a current acquaintance.
- Find yourself wanting to conceal from your partner certain friendships, purchases, or ways you spend your time.
- Wish your partner were as spiritual (or as friendly, as interesting) as you feel yourself to be, or as someone else's spouse whom you admire.
- Find the relationship with your spouse is suffering because one or more relatives has come to live in your home.

These vignettes are examples of nitty-gritty problems with which many Christian partners struggle. If not confronted and dealt with through prayer, asking and granting forgiveness and/or seeking godly counsel, such problems may start out seemingly small but end up consuming a relationship. They are footholds the devil will exploit in an effort to destroy marriages (see Ephesians 4:26-27).

GOD'S PLAN

Marriage, family, and home were God's plan from the beginning of creation. The second chapter of Genesis records his words after God had brought Adam into being: "It is not good for the man to be alone. I will make a helper suitable for him" (Genesis 2:18). Then God formed a woman from the rib he had taken out of the man. Adam expressed his delight. God blessed them and said, "Be fruitful and increase in number; fill the earth and subdue it..." (Genesis 1:28).

Since God initiated marriages, Satan does anything possible to interfere with godly marriages, and to damage relationships between righteous people.

PROTECTING YOUR MARRIAGE

Paul teaches that God intended marriage to be a picture of the relationship between Christ and his church (see Ephesians 5:21-23). Is it any wonder that Satan lashes out at marriages, trying to destroy them? Or that he tries to ravage the fruit of marriage, our children? God wants us to be aware of Satan's schemes and guard against them (see 2 Corinthians 2:11 and Ephesians 6:11).

Christian couples must make it a priority to pray together, to walk in mutual forgiveness, and to keep their communication with one another open and honest. Dr. Archibald Hart writes:

> If we are married, we need to focus on our marriage relationship. Since our relationship with our spouse is to be our sole sexual focus, this is where we need to direct our attention. Building a good marriage is hard work. Every marriage begins with the union of two incompatible people in an impossible relationship. The task God gives us in marriage is to turn it into something beautiful. With God's grace—it *can* be done.[1]

In God's design, the couple's sexual union causes them to "become one flesh" (Ephesians 5:31). That means being glued or cemented together. Concerning sexual relationships outside of marriage, Paul writes: "Do you not know that he who unites himself with a prostitute is one with her in body? For it is said, 'The two will become one flesh.'... Flee from sexual immorality.... he who sins sexually sins against his own body" (1 Corinthians 6:16, 18). His letter to the Hebrews puts it this way: "Marriage should be honored by all, and the marriage bed kept pure, for God will judge the adulterer and all the sexually immoral" (Hebrews 13:4).

Clearly, God desires that marriage partners be faithful to one another sexually. To protect them from attack in this area, wise believers know they must work at keeping the relationship strong spiritually and emotionally.

PRAYING FOR AN UNFAITHFUL PARTNER

While there is no *formula* for prayer, there are biblical examples that often give us strategies. One story tells of how God intervened on behalf of Hosea, a husband with a straying wife:

> ... She [Gomer] said, "I will go after my lovers,
>   who give me my food and my water,
>   my wool and my linen, my oil and my drink."
> Therefore I [God] will block her path with thornbushes;
>   I will wall her in so that she cannot find her way.
> She will chase after her lovers but not catch them;
>   she will look for them but not find them.
> Then she will say,
>   "I will go back to my husband as at first,
>   for then I was better off than now." **Hosea 2:5-7**

God told Hosea he would block Gomer's path with thorns so her lovers would lose interest in her. That's exactly what happened. God hedged her in and kept Gomer and her lovers from finding one another. That divine hedge was a protective barrier that resulted in Gomer's change of heart.

Hosea's story can serve as a pattern for those praying for unfaithful partners, or when praying for anyone in an adulterous relationship. No person can overcome a spouse's willful determination to pursue an adulterous affair. But we can ask God to intervene as only he is able. Pray that the Lord would arrest that person's attention, provide a barrier between the straying spouse and his or her lover, and place a strong believer in the wayward person's path to speak God's Word into the situation.

HOW TO REPAIR A BROKEN RELATIONSHIP

It is essential that an unfaithful partner who returns to his or her spouse break the unholy bonds established through any illicit sexual relationships. This is a suggested pattern:

1. Repent for breaking God's law. Ask God's forgiveness for each liaison, mentioning in prayer the names of those with whom you had sexual relationships outside marriage.
2. Declare in the name of Jesus that all past bondings are now broken and will no longer affect you.
3. Command all unclean spirits associated with past illicit relationships to leave you in the name of Jesus. The devil has no more rights in that area of your life because it is under the blood of Jesus.
4. Thank God for his forgiveness, his cleansing, and for your marriage partner who took you back.
5. Ask the Lord to strengthen you to walk in your freedom, and "not be entangled again with a yoke of bondage" (Galatians 5:1).[2]

FORGIVENESS BRINGS FREEDOM

Some families are constantly plagued with strife, resentment, anger, bitterness, or tension because one or more family member has opened a door to the enemy. Such divisiveness is often due to a person's own willful disobedience, rebellion, jealousy, immorality, involvement with the occult, idolatry, pride, selfishness, or substance abuse—to name only a few possible culprits. The enemy seizes any available foothold to gain access to our closest relationships.

While we can't force other people give up their choice to sin, we can prevent their disobedience from ruining our relationship with the Lord (and others) and robbing us of joy. The key factor in restoring any broken relationship is *forgiveness.*

No freedom can compare to that which comes when we decide to set at liberty anyone against whom we've held a grudge because of a hurt he or she inflicted on us. While releasing the other person from our judgment, forgiveness also sets us free from the poisonous sin of unforgiveness. That release allows God to deal more directly with the offender without interference.

One Bible teacher declared, "To forgive is like acquitting a defendant, clearing him even if he's guilty, and dealing with him as though innocent. It is freeing one as it were from prison, chains or bondage." Forgiveness carries a connected promise, as these verses illustrate: "Do not judge, and you will not be judged. Do not condemn, and you will not be condemned. Forgive, and you will be forgiven" (Luke 6:37). "For if you forgive men when they sin against you, your heavenly Father will also forgive you. But if you do not forgive men their sins, your Father will not forgive your sins" (Matthew 6:14-15).

Jesus died to cancel our huge debt of sin. If the Son of God could hang on a cross and say, "Father, forgive them," how can we not forgive the one who has wounded us? Ask the Lord to help you to make that choice. Forgiveness is an *act of the will,* not an *emotion.* When you choose to follow the example of Christ, he quickly comes to your aid.

Forgiveness also can be defined as unconditionally bestowing or granting our favor, or laying down our desire to get even. We see this perspective modeled in Paul's letter to the Ephesians: "Get rid of all bitterness, rage and anger, brawling and slander, along with every form of malice. Be kind and compassionate to one another, forgiving each other, just as in Christ God forgave you" (Ephesians 4:31-32).

After forgiveness has been freely bestowed, you and your spouse may need the help of a qualified counselor to restore your communication and rebuild trust. Unfortunately, some marriages do fail when both parties are not willing to work toward reconciliation. But even in a "worst case" scenario, God can strengthen and sustain you no matter what course of action your spouse may choose. (We discuss praying for marriages more fully in our books, *A Woman's Guide to Spiritual Warfare* and *How to Pray for Your Family and Friends.*)

If your family exhibits any specific pattern of sin (such as adultery, incest, witchcraft, addiction, etc.), you may need to break its power in prayer. Before he returned to Jerusalem to rebuild the demolished walls of his ancestor's homeland, Nehemiah wept, mourned, fasted, prayed, and confessed the sins of his forefathers (see Nehemiah 1:6-7).

PRAYER FOR BREAKING A SIN PATTERN

Father God, I confess before you the sins of my ancestors and ask you to have mercy on me and all members of my family. Forgive us for the sin of _____ that's been in our family for generations. Thank you that Jesus Christ came to set us free from the curse of the iniquities of our forefathers. I pray that each member of my family will receive the cleansing of the blood of Jesus and the deliverance he alone can give.

By the power and authority of Jesus Christ, I destroy that sin pattern of _____ and declare its curse broken. It has no more right to invade our family line. Thank you, Father, for the freedom that is ours through the shed blood of your son, Jesus Christ! Amen.

SCRIPTURES

Love is patient, love is kind. It does not envy, it does not boast, it is not proud. It is not rude, it is not self-seeking, it is not easily angered, it keeps no record of wrongs. Love does not delight in evil but rejoices with the truth. It always protects, always trusts, always hopes, always perseveres.   1 Corinthians 13:4-7

Now to him who is able to do immeasurably more than all we ask or imagine, according to his power that is at work within us, to him be glory in the church and in Christ Jesus throughout all generations, for ever and ever! Amen.   Ephesians 3:20-21

Unless the LORD builds the house,
    its builders labor in vain....   Psalm 127:1

Marry and have sons and daughters; find wives for your sons and give your daughters in marriage, so that they too may have sons and daughters. Increase in number there; do not decrease.   Jeremiah 29:6

WIVES AND HUSBANDS

He who finds a wife finds what is good
    and receives favor from the LORD.   Proverbs 18:22

For this reason a man will leave his father and mother and be united to his wife, and the two will become one flesh.

Ephesians 5:31

Wives, submit to your husbands as to the Lord. For the husband is the head of the wife as Christ is the head of the church, his body, of which he is the Savior. Now as the church submits to Christ, so also wives should submit to their husbands in everything.
    Husbands, love your wives, just as Christ loved the church and gave himself up for her to make her holy, cleansing her by the washing with water through the word, and to present

her to himself as a radiant church, without stain or wrinkle or any other blemish, but holy and blameless. In this same way, husbands ought to love their wives as their own bodies. He who loves his wife loves himself.   **Ephesians 5:22-28**

May your fountain be blessed,
    and may you rejoice in the wife of your youth.   **Proverbs 5:18**

Why be captivated, my son, by an adulteress?
Why embrace the bosom of another man's wife?   **Proverbs 5:20**

Houses and wealth are inherited from parents,
    but a prudent wife is from the LORD.   **Proverbs 19:14**

A wife of noble character who can find?
    She is worth far more than rubies....
Her children arise and call her blessed;
    her husband also, and he praises her:
"Many women do noble things,
    but you surpass them all."   **Proverbs 31:10, 28-29**

... the LORD is acting as the witness between you and the wife of your youth, because you have broken faith with her, though she is your partner, the wife of your marriage covenant. Has not [the LORD] made them one? In flesh and spirit they are his. And why one? Because he was seeking godly offspring. So guard yourself in your spirit, and do not break faith with the wife of your youth.   **Malachi 2:14-15**

"It has been said, 'Anyone who divorces his wife must give her a certificate of divorce.' But I [Jesus] tell you that anyone who divorces his wife, except for marital unfaithfulness, causes her to become an adulteress, and anyone who marries the divorced woman commits adultery."   **Matthew 5:31-32**

[Jesus replied,] "For this reason a man will leave his father and mother and be united to his wife, and the two will become one flesh. So they are no longer two, but one. Therefore what God has joined together, let man not separate."   **Mark 10:7-9**

The husband should fulfill his marital duty to his wife, and likewise the wife to her husband. The wife's body does not belong to her alone but also to her husband. In the same way, the husband's body does not belong to him alone but also to his wife. 1 Corinthians 7:3-4

To the married I give this command (not I [Paul], but the Lord): A wife must not separate from her husband. But if she does, she must remain unmarried or else be reconciled to her husband. And a husband must not divorce his wife.

1 Corinthians 7:10-11

For the unbelieving husband has been sanctified through his wife, and the unbelieving wife has been sanctified through her believing husband. Otherwise your children would be unclean, but as it is, they are holy. 1 Corinthians 7:14

A woman is bound to her husband as long as he lives. But if her husband dies, she is free to marry anyone she wishes, but he must belong to the Lord. 1 Corinthians 7:39

FOR WIVES TO PRAY

Lord, I desire to be the helper for my husband that you want me to be and that he needs. May I do him good all the days of his life and may he have full confidence in me. I want to watch over the affairs of our household wisely. Lord, help us to mutually respect and love one another. May our home be a place of peace and security where you are honored and worshiped. I ask in Jesus' name. Amen.

FOR HUSBANDS TO PRAY

Lord, may I love my wife as Jesus loved the church. I thank you for this special woman you have provided for me. Help me to show her how much I love and appreciate and cherish her. May I be a good provider in every area of her life. Help us to serve you together, Father, and to be a godly example to our children. In Jesus' name, Amen.

A PRAYER FOR A BELIEVING SPOUSE

May God himself, the God of peace, sanctify you through and through. May your whole spirit, soul and body be kept blameless at the coming of our Lord Jesus Christ. The one who calls you is faithful and he will do it.   **1 Thessalonians 5:23-24**

A PRAYER FOR AN UNBELIEVING SPOUSE

... [that] God will grant them repentance leading them to a knowledge of the truth, and that they will come to their senses and escape from the trap of the devil, who has taken them captive to do his will.   **2 Timothy 2:25-26**

... open their eyes and turn them from darkness to light, and from the power of Satan to God, so that they may receive forgiveness of sins and a place among those who are sanctified by faith in me [Jesus].   **Acts 26:18**

SCRIPTURES ON STRIFE

"For by your words you will be acquitted, and by your words you will be condemned".   **Matthew 12:37**

Above all else, guard your heart,
    for it is the wellspring of life.
Put away perversity from your mouth;
    keep corrupt talk far from your lips.   **Proverbs 4:23-24**

If you have been trapped by what you said,
    ensnared by the words of your mouth,
then do this, my son, to free yourself,
    since you have fallen into your neighbor's hands:

Go and humble yourself;
    press your plea with your neighbor!
Allow no sleep to your eyes,
    no slumber to your eyelids. **Proverbs 6:2-3**

When words are many, sin is not absent,
    but he who holds his tongue is wise. **Proverbs 10:19**

A gentle answer turns away wrath,
    but a harsh word stirs up anger....
He who guards his mouth and his tongue
    keeps himself from calamity. **Proverbs 15:1; 21:23**

My dear brothers, take note of this: Everyone should be quick
to listen, slow to speak and slow to become angry. **James 1:19**

Turn from evil and do good;
    seek peace and pursue it. **Psalm 34:14**

Set a guard over my mouth, O LORD;
    keep watch over the door of my lips. **Psalm 141:3**

If it is possible, as far as it depends on you, live at peace with
everyone. **Romans 12:18**

Do nothing out of selfish ambition or vain conceit, but in
humility consider others better than yourselves. Each of you
should look not only to your own interests, but also to the
interests of others. Your attitude should be the same as that of
Christ Jesus. **Philippians 2:3-5a**

To this you were called, because Christ suffered for you, leaving you an example, that you should follow in his steps.
    "He committed no sin,
        and no deceit was found in his mouth." **1 Peter 2:21-22**

A PRAYER AGAINST STRIFE

Lord, give me the wisdom to help repair breaches and mend broken relationships. May I not be a party to dissension and strife. I want to be pleasing to you, as well as a good example to others. Keep my mouth from deceit and malice. Help me, with the strength only you can provide, to walk in forgiveness. Amen.

16

Standing for Your Children

C HILDREN ARE A PRICELESS GIFT, a heritage from the Lord. What a privilege to stand in the gap for them, praying that they will achieve God's full potential.

God has cared deeply about families since he first brought Adam and Eve together. When he destroyed the earth with a flood because of humanity's wickedness, he chose to spare Noah and his family. Just as their salvation hinged upon their entering the door of the ark, so our families have one door of entrance—Jesus Christ.

As parents, we resonate with Joshua's cry: "... But as for me and my household, we will serve the LORD" (Joshua 24:15). Even if you aren't a parent, God may want you to stand in the prayer gap for children—perhaps those who have no one interceding for them. Helpless children are everywhere—in schools, churches, neighborhoods, streets, subways, buses, shopping malls, beaches, parks. Children in need of a Savior. But your prayers can make a difference.

PERSONALIZING SCRIPTURE

One especially effective spiritual warfare tactic involves personalizing verses of Scripture as you pray, such as replacing the pronouns with the names of the children or people for whom you're interceding. For example, Psalm 23:3 could be personalized in this way: "Thank you, Lord, that you guide my son Keith in the paths of righteousness for your name's sake." The verse takes on added potency as both an expression of praise to the Lord and a declaration of truth to the enemy.

We pray differently for children during various phases of their lives. For instance, the following prayer for a child who is either a student or an employee combines several verses:

> Lord, may my child like Daniel show "... aptitude for every kind of learning, [be] well informed, quick to understand and qualified to serve in the king's palace" (Daniel 1:4). May he/she "speak with wisdom and tact," and may he/she be "found to have a keen mind and knowledge and understanding and also the ability... to solve difficult problems" (Daniel 2:14; 5:12). Lord, endow my child with "wisdom and very great insight, and a breadth of understanding as measureless as the sand on the seashore" (1 Kings 4:29).

Another way to personalize these same Scripture verses would be to speak them aloud about your child: "My child will be found to have a keen mind and knowledge and understanding and ability to solve difficult problems. He/she does have wisdom and insight and breadth of understanding as measureless as the sand on the seashore." By hearing the Word of God—even from our own lips—we stand firm on his truth as applied in our very own family. Not only have we strengthened our own faith, we have also delivered a blow to the kingdom of darkness.

SCRIPTURES CONCERNING SPIRITUAL GROWTH

Thank you, Lord, that you know the plans you have for my child, "plans to prosper [my child] and not to harm [him/her], plans to give [child's name] a hope and a future" (Jeremiah 29:11).

May my child "live a life worthy of the Lord and please you in every way: bearing fruit in every good work, growing in the knowledge of God, being strengthened with all power according to your glorious might so that [child's name] may have great endurance and patience, and joyfully give thanks to the Father, who has qualified [him/her] to share in the inheritance of the saints in the kingdom of light. For he has rescued [my child] from the dominion of darkness and brought [him/her] into the kingdom of the Son he loves, in whom [child's name] has redemption, the forgiveness of sins" (Colossians 1:10-14).

DRAWING UP BATTLE PLANS

All children need prayer, be they wayward or godly. But the types of prayers will differ according to specific circumstances. Biblical battles were not all fought with the same strategy. Similarly, we seek *God's battle plan* when praying for our children, asking him to reveal appropriate Scriptures for each particular situation.

Let's consider how you might pray for a child who is being adversely influenced by peers. God may:

1. Lead you to pray as David did when he believed his son Absalom was hearing the wrong advice. He asked the Lord to "turn [the] counsel into foolishness" (2 Samuel 15:31).

2. He may lead you to pray that your child be "delivered from wicked and evil men," and that God would "strengthen and protect [him/her] from the evil one." (2 Thessalonians 3:2, 3).

3. Or God may want you to bless that person, even when your natural inclination is to ask God to remove that harmful influence from your child's life. You can pray that God will accomplish his plan and purpose in that person, bringing the right people into his or her life at the right time (see Ephesians 1:11; Matthew 9:38). God broke Job's captivity when he prayed for his friends, and they weren't exactly the kind of friends most of us would want (Job 42:10).

4. God may lead you to many other Scriptures, some listed in this chapter.

GODLY GOALS

What does God desire for our children? Scripture provides many answers concerning the heart of our heavenly Father toward his little ones.

1. That Jesus Christ be formed in our children (see Galatians 4:19).

2. That our children—the seed of the righteous—will be delivered from the evil one (see Proverbs 11:21 KJV; Matthew 6:13).

3. That our children will be taught of the Lord and their peace will be great (see Isaiah 54:13).

4. That they will train themselves to discern good from evil and have a good conscience toward God (see Hebrews 5:14; 1 Peter 3:21).

5. That God's laws will be in their minds and on their hearts (see Hebrews 8:10).

6. That they will choose companions who are wise—not fools, nor sexually immoral, nor drunkards, nor idol-

aters, nor slanderers, nor swindlers (see Proverbs 13:20;
1 Corinthians 5:11).
7. That they will remain sexually pure and keep themselves
only for their spouse, asking God for his grace to keep
such a commitment (see Ephesians 5:3, 31-33).
8. That they will honor their parents (Ephesians 6:1-3).

Many other Scriptures could be added to this list, one
which will change over time as God shows you new ways to
pray his Word. Ask God for specific promises to stand on during difficult situations.

OTHER SCRIPTURES

"… Remember the Lord, who is great and awesome, and fight
for your brothers, your sons and your daughters, your wives
and your homes." **Nehemiah 4:14**

The children of your servants will live in your presence;
their descendants will be established before you. **Psalm 102:28**

But from everlasting to everlasting
the LORD's love is with those who fear him,
and his righteousness with their children's children—
with those who keep his covenant
and remember to obey his precepts. **Psalm 103:17**

"All your sons will be taught by the LORD,
and great will be your children's peace.…
no weapon forged against you will prevail,
and you will refute every tongue that accuses you.
This is the heritage of the servants of the LORD,
and this is their vindication from me,"
declares the LORD. **Isaiah 54:13, 17**

Know therefore that the LORD your God is God; he is the
faithful God, keeping his covenant of love to a thousand gen-

erations of those who love him and keep his commands.
Deuteronomy 7:9

Do not be afraid, for I am with you;
   I will bring your children from the east
   and gather you from the west....
For I will pour water on the thirsty land,
   and streams on the dry ground;
I will pour out my Spirit on your offspring,
   and my blessing on your descendants. **Isaiah 43:5; 44:3**

He who fears the LORD has a secure fortress,
   and for his children it will be a refuge. **Proverbs 14:26**

"... I will pour out my Spirit on all people.
Your sons and daughters will prophesy...." **Joel 2:28**

The promise [of the Holy Spirit] is for you and your children and for all who are far off—for all whom the Lord our God will call. **Acts 2:39**

But this is what the LORD says:
"... I will contend with those who contend with you,
   and your children I will save." **Isaiah 49:25**

"As for me, this is my covenant with them," says the LORD. "My Spirit, who is on you, and my words that I have put in your mouth will not depart from your mouth, or from the mouths of your children, or from the mouths of their descendants from this time on and forever," says the LORD. **Isaiah 59:21**

This is what the LORD says:
"Restrain your voice from weeping
   and your eyes from tears,
for your work will be rewarded,"
     declares the LORD.

"They will return from the land of the enemy.
So there is hope for your future," declares the LORD.
   "Your children will return to their own land." **Jeremiah 31:16-17**

Sons are a heritage from the LORD,
   children a reward from him. **Psalm 127:3**

Train a child in the way he should go,
   and when he is old he will not turn from it. **Proverbs 22:6**

He will turn the hearts of the fathers to their children, and
the hearts of the children to their fathers.... **Malachi 4:6**

"And lead us not into temptation,
but deliver us from the evil one." **Matthew 6:13**

"Ask the Lord of the harvest, therefore, to send out workers
into his harvest field." **Matthew 9:38**

I have not stopped giving thanks for you, remembering you in
my prayers. I keep asking that the God of our Lord Jesus
Christ, the glorious Father, may give you the Spirit of wisdom
and revelation, so that you may know him better. I pray also
that the eyes of your heart may be enlightened in order that
you may know the hope to which he has called you, the riches
of his glorious inheritance in the saints, and his incomparably
great power.... **Ephesians 1:16-19**

I pray that out of his glorious riches he may strengthen you
with power through his Spirit in your inner being, so that
Christ may dwell in your hearts through faith. And I pray that
you, being rooted and established in love, may have power,...
to grasp how wide and long and high and deep is the love of
Christ, and to know this love that surpasses knowledge—that
you may be filled to the measure of all the fullness of God.

                                     Ephesians 3:16-19

HEALING FOR CHILDREN

... A ruler came and knelt before him and said, "My daughter has just died. But come and put your hand on her, and she will live." Jesus got up and went with him, and so did his disciples....

When Jesus entered the ruler's house and saw the flute players and the noisy crowd, he said, "Go away. The girl is not dead but asleep." But they laughed at him. After the crowd had been put outside, he went in and took the girl by the hand, and she got up. **Matthew 9:18-19, 23-25**

"Lord, have mercy on my son," he said. "He has seizures and is suffering greatly. He often falls into the fire or into the water."... Jesus rebuked the demon, and it came out of the boy, and he was healed from that moment. **Matthew 17:15, 18**

... And there was a certain royal officer whose son lay sick at Capernaum. When this man heard that Jesus had arrived in Galilee from Judea, he went to him and begged him to come and heal his son, who was close to death....

"Sir, come down before my child dies."

Jesus replied, "You may go. Your son will live."

The man took Jesus at his word and departed. While he was still on the way, his servants met him with the news that his boy was living....

Then the father realized that this was the exact time at which Jesus had said to him, "Your son will live." So he and all his household believed. **John 4:46-53**

SCRIPTURES FOR SALVATION

Surely the arm of the LORD is not too short to save,
    nor his ear too dull to hear. **Isaiah 59:1**

..."Believe in the Lord Jesus, and you will be saved—you and your household." **Acts 16:31**

... I am sending you to them to open their eyes and turn them from darkness to light, and from the power of Satan to God, so that they may receive forgiveness of sins and a place among those who are sanctified by faith in me [Jesus].

Acts 26:17-18

... do you show contempt for the riches of his kindness, tolerance and patience, not realizing that God's kindness leads you toward repentance? **Romans 2:4**

... God our Savior... wants all men to be saved and to come to a knowledge of the truth. **1 Timothy 2:3-4**

... God... grant them repentance leading them to a knowledge of the truth, [so] that they will come to their senses and escape from the trap of the devil, who has taken them captive to do his will. **2 Timothy 2:25-26**

The Lord is not slow in keeping his promise, as some understand slowness. He is patient with you, not wanting anyone to perish, but everyone to come to repentance. **2 Peter 3:9**

A DECLARATION OF FAITH TO THE ENEMY

Devil, the Word of God says you have held my child captive to do your will. In the name of the Lord Jesus Christ of Nazareth to whom I belong, I bind your power and tell you to loose my child's will, leaving him free to choose Jesus and his plan for [child's name] life. Jesus' blood was shed for him/her.

My child will come to his/her senses and escape from your trap. My child's eyes will be opened and he/she will turn from darkness to light, translated from Satan's kingdom to God's kingdom. [Child's name] will receive forgiveness of sins and a place among those sanctified in the Lord Jesus. I believe in the Lord Jesus, and my household will be saved.

PRAYER FOR OUR CHILDREN

Thank you, Lord, that you will contend with those who contend with me, and you will save my children. Thank you that you will bring those back from the land of the enemy who have strayed. I rejoice in your promises for them. Thank you for the gift of these precious children. Amen.

Parents are justly concerned about their children marrying godly spouses. It should be a prayer priority. Following are suggested prayers for parents to pray for a single son or daughter (actually prayed by a father).

PRAYER FOR A DAUGHTER'S FUTURE HUSBAND

The father of a thirty-two-year-old single (never married) prays:

Lord, I ask you to release the man you have preordained as my daughter's husband. May he come forth soon to ask me for her hand in marriage. May he love you with all his heart and embrace Jesus as his personal Savior. May he love his wife as Christ loves the church and establish their home in accordance with Ephesians 5:20-28.

Lord, years ago you gave her a verse for her future husband (a description of the youthful David). Because you gave her this word, I stand with her for a husband who is "a skillful musician, a mighty man of valor, a warrior, one prudent in speech, and a handsome man; and the Lord is with him" (1 Samuel 16:18b NAS).

Father, if the enemy is keeping them from meeting and marrying, I ask you to send forth mighty angels to do battle on their behalf. I believe you have created my daughter for a special man of God. I stand in the gap and call him forth out of obscurity into her life. Don't let the enemy send a counterfeit. Thank you for my future son-in-law.

Continue your work in my daughter to make her content until he comes. Thank you, Lord, for her talents and gifts that she now uses in your kingdom's work that will complement the talents of the man you have groomed for her. I pronounce a priestly blessing upon their union and future offspring, and thank you in advance for what you have planned for them. Amen.

PRAYER FOR A SON'S FUTURE WIFE

Father God, just as Abraham sent his servant to find his son Isaac a wife, please send the Holy Spirit to bring my son's future wife to him. May she have the needed attributes of the Proverbs 31 woman so she will be both a godly wife and a godly mother. Give them supernatural love for one another. May they both love and serve the Lord Jesus Christ all their days. Thank you for the call of God on their lives.

Lord, don't allow the enemy to keep them apart. Fulfill your purpose for them by bringing them together. Thank you for the Christian girl you've been preparing all these years for my son. Help us receive her as our own daughter, and help her to receive us as parents.

Thank you for pouring out your blessings upon them and meeting all their needs. Thank you for making them sensitive to your guidance and your timing for their marriage. I pray they will bring forth godly offspring who will serve you and glorify your name. Amen.

17

Fighting against Childlessness or Abortion

"**B**E FRUITFUL AND MULTIPLY," the Lord commanded Adam and Eve. When a couple becomes one in flesh and spirit through marriage, God normally intends for them to produce godly offspring (see Genesis 1:28; Malachi 2:15).

Married men and women usually experience a longing to fulfill their God-given desire to have children together. But sometimes the desired pregnancy does not happen so easily as they hoped. Infertility actually afflicts about 15 percent of couples, and may involve either the man or the woman, or both. Doctors may be able to help, but God is ever ready to hear our cry of need.

Perhaps no other woman cried out so much for a baby as did Hannah. God eventually gave her and her husband many children after she had given her firstborn, Samuel, to the

Lord. Samuel later became a great prophet of God. These are Hannah's words of dedication: "I prayed for this child, and the LORD has granted me what I asked of him. So now I give him to the LORD..." (1 Samuel 1:27-28).

In the biblical examples of God's intervention on behalf of childless couples, we can make three observations:

1. God gave them a child as a promise.
2. God answered the prayers of the wife or husband.
3. God gave them children because it was his intention for them to have a family. Today God is performing miracles to give children to couples struggling with infertility.

Specifically praying for God to help you conceive a child acknowledges the Creator as the source of life, as well as the One to praise and honor when the birth occurs. Satan, on the other hand, does everything he can to frustrate conception, thus eliminating potential godly offspring. He often perverts sex, plants unbelief and fear, and scrambles communication between spouses.

The difficulty can sometimes be more spiritual in nature. Couples unable to produce children might further consider whether they have displeased God by bringing false gods or occult objects into their home or if they have subjected themselves to a curse by engaging in forbidden practices recorded in God's Word. (See Deuteronomy 27-28 and other teaching on the occult in this book.)

If so, the couple needs to destroy any such objects and repent of the forbidden acts, as well as renounce any curse or ties with Satan or the occult. They can then accept the Lord's forgiveness and thank him that "Christ redeemed us from the curse of the law by becoming a curse for us..." (Galatians 3:13). The following statement may be helpful:

We renounce all ties and association with occult practices and the works of darkness, and declare they have no power over us. We submit ourselves to the Lordship of Jesus

Christ, and apply the blood of Jesus to our lives and our marriage relationship.

Don't let the enemy or other people inflict guilt or condemnation upon you if you have been unable to produce children. God can use your talents and love for his little ones in many creative ways. When a married couple yearns for a child, what encouragement they gain by reading aloud God's Word as they stand in faith for a baby.

HOPE FOR CHILDLESSNESS

"Worship the LORD your God, and his blessing will be on your food and water. I will take away sickness from among you, and none will miscarry or be barren in your land. I will give you a full life span." **Exodus 23:25**

Now the LORD was gracious to Sarah as he had said, and the LORD did for Sarah what he had promised. Sarah became pregnant and bore a son to Abraham in his old age, at the very time God had promised him. **Genesis 21:1-2**

By faith Abraham, even though he was past age—and Sarah herself was barren—was enabled to become a father because he considered him faithful who had made the promise. And so from this one man, and he as good as dead, came descendants as numerous as the stars in the sky and as countless as the sand on the seashore. **Hebrews 11:11-12**

A certain man of Zorah, named Manoah, from the clan of the Danites, had a wife who was sterile and remained childless. The angel of the LORD appeared to her and said, "You are sterile and childless, but you are going to conceive and have a son. Now see to it that you drink no wine or other fermented drink and that you do not eat anything unclean, because you will conceive and give birth to a son. No razor may be used on

his head, because the boy is to be a Nazirite, set apart to God
from birth, and he will begin the deliverance of Israel from
the hands of the Philistines."...

The woman gave birth to a boy and named him Samson.
He grew and the LORD blessed him.... Judges 13:2-5, 24

In bitterness of soul Hannah wept much and prayed to the
LORD. And she made a vow, saying, "O LORD Almighty, if you
will only look upon your servant's misery and remember me,
and not forget your servant but give her a son, then I will give
him to the LORD for all the days of his life, and no razor will
ever be used on his head."

"... I prayed for this child, and the LORD has granted me
what I asked of him. So now I give him to the LORD. For his
whole life he will be given over to the LORD." 1 Samuel 1:10-11, 27-28

Then Hannah prayed and said:
    "My heart rejoices in the LORD;
        in the LORD my horn is lifted high.
    My mouth boasts over my enemies,
        for I delight in your deliverance....
    She who was barren has borne seven children...."
                                        1 Samuel 2:1, 5b

Eli would bless Elkanah and his wife, saying, "May the LORD
give you children by this woman to take the place of the one
she prayed for and gave to the LORD." Then they would go
home. And the LORD was gracious to Hannah; she conceived
and gave birth to three sons and two daughters. Meanwhile,
the boy Samuel grew up in the presence of the LORD.
                                        1 Samuel 2:20-21

Isaac prayed to the LORD on behalf of his wife, because she
was barren. The LORD answered his prayer, and his wife
Rebekah became pregnant. Genesis 25:21

So Boaz took Ruth and she became his wife.... And the LORD
enabled her to conceive, and she gave birth to a son. The

women said to Naomi: "Praise be to the LORD, who this day has not left you without a kinsman-redeemer. May he become famous throughout Israel! He will renew your life and sustain you in your old age. For your daughter-in-law, who loves you and who is better to you than seven sons, has given him birth." Ruth 4:13-15

Then an angel of the Lord appeared to him... "Do not be afraid, Zechariah; your prayer has been heard. Your wife Elizabeth will bear you a son, and you are to give him the name John. He will be a joy and delight to you, and many will rejoice because of his birth, for he will be great in the sight of the Lord...."

After this his wife Elizabeth became pregnant and for five months remained in seclusion. "The Lord has done this for me," she said. "In these days he has shown his favor and taken away my disgrace among the people." Luke 1:11-15, 24-25

He settles the barren woman in her home
    as a happy mother of children.
Praise the LORD. Psalm 113:9

Blessed are all who fear the LORD,
    who walk in his ways....
Your wife will be like a fruitful vine
    within your house;
your sons will be like olive shoots
    around your table. Psalm 128:1, 3

If you fully obey the LORD your God and carefully follow all his commands I give you today, the LORD your God will set you high above all the nations on earth. All these blessings will come upon you and accompany you if you obey the LORD your God:

    You will be blessed in the city and blessed in the country.

    The fruit of your womb will be blessed.... Deuteronomy 28:1-3, 4

For you created my inmost being;
  you knit me together in my mother's womb. **Psalm 139:13**

When Elizabeth heard Mary's greeting, the baby leaped in her womb, and Elizabeth was filled with the Holy Spirit.
  Luke 1:41

Now to him who is able to do immeasurably more than all we ask or imagine, according to his power that is at work within us, to him be glory in the church and in Christ Jesus throughout all generations, for ever and ever! Amen. **Ephesians 3:20-21**

"I am the LORD, the God of all mankind. Is anything too hard for me?" **Jeremiah 32:27**

A SPIRIT OF MURDER

Because life is so precious to God, he is grieved over abortion or murder in the womb. Jesus himself says the devil was a murderer from the beginning (John 8:44), so having an abortion means cooperating with a spirit of murder. Clearly, the consequences are grave.

Says Gary L. Bauer, president of Family Research Council for Focus on the Family:

Abortion is the most radical smashing of the parent-child bond that mankind in his wickedness has ever come up with. It is not just saying no to pregnancy now so as to say yes to it later. It is saying no, forever, to a particular individual, and unrepeatable little human being, who has already commenced biological existence.[1]

Consider these facts: A baby's heart is beating twenty-five days after conception. Brain waves can be recorded in forty-five days. By the eighth week, the baby in the womb responds to touch and pain.[2]

A woman who has had an abortion needs deliverance from a spirit of murder or destruction. She needs to confess her abortion as sin to God the Father, ask his forgiveness, and receive his cleansing. Then she needs to forgive herself and receive God's healing.

If you have harshly judged someone for having an abortion, remember their own excruciating pain when they realize the significance of their decision. They need our help, not our rejection. These Scriptures may be useful in spiritual warfare on their behalf:

Let no one be found among you who sacrifices his son or daughter in the fire.... **Deuteronomy 18:10**

I am forgotten by them as though I were dead;
I have become like broken pottery.
For I hear the slander of many;
   there is terror on every side;
they conspire against me
   and plot to take my life. **Psalm 31:12-13**

"But that you may know that the Son of Man has authority on earth to forgive sins...." **Mark 2:10a**

18

Victorious and Single

WHILE GOD LONGS TO GIVE US a fulfilling life, Satan wants just the opposite. Some singles believe they will only be complete and useful to the Lord if and when they find a husband or wife. Not so! Don't yield to that lie of the enemy. Single adults—whether never-married, widowed, or divorced —are whole persons in themselves whom God can use in many ways to build his kingdom.

Singleness is not an obstacle to victory in the Lord. Nor is it a problem to be solved. Some of Satan's tactics against godly singles include:

- Harrassing them with chronic discontent so that they are unable to serve God joyfully while single.
- Attacking their chastity by luring them into unholy and unhealthy alliances.
- Trying to keep them from maintaining a pure and close relationship with the Lord.

- Convincing them to believe the lie that without marriage they will remain incomplete and unfulfilled.

The apostle Paul had a word for singles in relationship to their opportunity to serve the Lord. He wrote:

> I would like you to be free from concern. An unmarried man is concerned about the Lord's affairs—how he can please the Lord. But a married man is concerned about the affairs of this world—how he can please his wife—and his interests are divided. An unmarried woman or virgin is concerned about the Lord's affairs: Her aim is to be devoted to the Lord in both body and spirit. But a married woman is concerned about the affairs of this world—how she can please her husband. I am saying this for your own good, not to restrict you, but that you may live in a right way in undivided devotion to the Lord.   1 Corinthians 7:32-35

Paul does not say marriage is wrong. Rather, he advises a single person to spend "undivided devotion" to the Lord—total commitment and concentration upon the Lord. To please the Lord in every way—less concerned about the affairs of the world—is both a challenge and opportunity to the unmarried Christian.

Michael Cavanaugh, who founded Mobilized to Serve, an international ministry to single adults, and has written *God's Call to the Single Adult* says:

> Your singleness is a gift from God for service. As in no other time in your life, your season as a single person sets you free to serve God in a wholehearted and undistracted way. Unencumbered by many of the duties and responsibilities that go along with the married life, you are able to say "yes" to God in a dynamic way. You are free to throw yourself with abandon into the things of God—to know Him as you have never known Him before, to love Him in an intimate way, and to serve Him with all your heart, soul, mind and strength—one hundred percent.[1]

Speaking to the student body at Christ for the Nations Institute, he shared some of the following truths:

1. In Christ you have been made complete (see Colossians 2:10). Jesus came to give you a full life right now. No human can give you worth or value except Jesus. To prepare for marriage, become the mightiest single person you can be for Jesus!
2. Recognize that marriage is not God's ultimate will for your life; it is to be conformed to the likeness of his son, Jesus (see Romans 8:29).
3. Your present singleness is the result of your choices. You could have married someone without standards. But you have chosen certain standards—to follow Jesus.
4. Singleness is a gift from God for service, whether temporary or permanent. It's a gift of grace to walk victoriously in this season of your life while he is building his character in you.[2]

Jesus, in discussing marriage with his disciples, reminded them that in the beginning the Creator made them male and female. "... For this reason a man will leave his father and mother and be united to his wife, and the two will become one flesh.... Therefore what God has joined together, let man not separate." Then he added: "... others have renounced marriage because of the kingdom of heaven..." (Matthew 19:5a, 6b, 12b).

Some men and women will remain single for life. Perhaps such a commitment will enable them to undertake a particular service for the Lord with greater freedom. Be attentive to the Lord and how he wants to guide your life.

God may direct you to lay certain relationships at the foot of the cross because he knows in the end it will be damaging, not beneficial. The Holy Spirit gives comfort, strength and wisdom to those who obey this call. You can absolutely trust your future to the One who has your best interests at heart.

If you feel God does desire you to be married, it is still

important to give wholehearted devotion to the Lord in the waiting period. Go where he wants you to go. Do what he wants you to do. Live life to the fullest, without thinking marriage is the answer to all your problems.

In his book, *Singles Plus,* Ray Mossholder discusses the single life from a biblical perspective. One comment: "You should always be able to give God and yourself a good reason why you are dating someone. Be honest about it. You should follow this simple rule: I will always keep pure motives for dating."[3]

What are the right reasons for marrying? Mossholder writes: "Perhaps the 'rightest' is so the two of you can serve Jesus Christ better together than you could if you were single. Secondary reasons include love, companionship, sharing, the strength of prayer when two pray, the joy of rearing children together and the fulfillment of God-blessed sex."[4]

WAITING ON GOD

Suppose God has planted a desire in your heart for a spouse. How can you combat temptation or impure thoughts while single? The answer sounds simple but requires discipline. Every time the enemy tries to make you feel sorry for yourself or urges you to indulge in sex outside of marriage, take authority over the enemy by audibly repeating the Word of God.

Maybe you feel you are in a "waiting stage" before your spouse comes along. What do you do? Pray. Wait for his timing and be content in him. Don't panic. Total commitment means trusting the Lord's plan and timing for your life. Whether single or married, fulfilling God's purpose for our life is of paramount importance.

DON'T ALLOW SATAN TO SIDETRACK GOD'S PLAN

Since God initiated family life, his archenemy Satan does anything he can to interfere with godly marriages, and to sabotage relationships between righteous people. Several pastors believe that Satan not only wants to kill babies through abortion but also wants to keep godly men and women from meeting, marrying, and producing godly offspring. In recent years these pastors have noticed men in their congregations fearing commitment, or women panicking because they see no potential marriage partner.

Dr. Archibald Hart, a Christian psychologist, talks about men whose parents divorced and are now themselves often hesitant about marriage. However, some of what he says easily applies to others unwilling to make commitments:

> "Don't make commitments" is a life motto for many male adult children of divorce. This means that commitments of a personal nature should be avoided, so many of these men make heroic efforts to avoid being "tied down." This effort may involve many aspects of life—such as renting instead of buying or moving from job to job. But by far the most common result of this life-script is avoidance of commitment to relationships. These men typically put off marriage as long as possible—or avoid it altogether. The decision to live together without marriage is often a consequence of this life-script. So are quick divorces. The sheer disposability of marriage breeds a faulty attitude toward commitment.
>
> ... In addition, he has probably picked up the "don't get tied down" message from the culture around him.... If you never commit yourself to anyone, you never get hurt.[5]

Seeing some men's tendency to delay marriage as a tactic of the enemy, one pastor suggested an aggressive retaliation: calling for God's plan to come forth, much as Jesus called Lazarus from the grave. "Remind the enemy that the Lord can do all things and no plan of his will be thwarted in your life," he said.

Another pastor uses this verse as a basis for prayer: "... Therefore what God has joined together, let man not separate" (Matthew 19:6). On behalf of some single sister, he would boldly proclaim: "Satan, you and your demons will not use any human to separate (name of person) and her future husband from meeting and marrying and producing godly children. What God has intended to join together, man will not separate. I break your power in Jesus' name. You loose your hold—they will meet and marry." Then this pastor thanks God that the Holy Spirit will draw them together, direct their meeting, dating, and marriage.

SCRIPTURES

Many are the plans in a man's heart,
  but it is the LORD's purpose that prevails.   **Proverbs 19:21**

The LORD will fulfill his purpose for me;
  your love, O LORD, endures forever—
    do not abandon the works of your hands.   **Psalm 138:8**

Whether you turn to the right or to the left, your ears will hear a voice behind you, saying, "This is the way; walk in it."
                                                        Isaiah 30:21

… as a bridegroom rejoices over his bride,
  so will your God rejoice over you.   **Isaiah 62:5**

"Sing, O Daughter of Zion;
  shout aloud, O Israel;
Be glad and rejoice with all your heart,
  O Daughter of Jerusalem!…
The LORD your God is with you,
  he is mighty to save.
He will take great delight in you,
  he will quiet you with his love,
    he will rejoice over you with singing."   **Zephaniah 3:14, 17**

But he who unites himself with the Lord is one with him in spirit.

Flee from sexual immorality.... Do you not know that your body is a temple of the Holy Spirit, who is in you, whom you have received from God? You are not your own; you were bought at a price. Therefore honor God with your body.

1 Corinthians 6:17-20

Flee the evil desires of youth, and pursue righteousness, faith, love and peace, along with those who call on the Lord out of a pure heart.   2 Timothy 2:22

Find rest, O my soul, in God alone;
    my hope comes from him.   Psalm 62:5

But godliness with contentment is great gain.   1 Timothy 6:6

... being confident of this, that he who began a good work in you will carry it on to completion until the day of Christ Jesus.

Philippians 1:6

I have learned the secret of being content in any and every situation, whether well fed or hungry, whether living in plenty or in want. I can do everything through him who gives me strength.   Philippians 4: 12b-13

Commit to the LORD whatever you do,
    and your plans will succeed.   Proverbs 16:3

Trust in the LORD with all your heart
    and lean not on your own understanding;
in all your ways acknowledge him,
    and he will make your paths straight.   Proverbs 3:5, 6

PRAYER FOR A SINGLE ADULT

Lord, thank you that I am complete in you. Thank you that you are conforming me to your image. Thank you for your mercy and grace that enable me to keep myself pure. My desire is to please you more than anyone; help me to do that, Lord. If there are relationships in my life that you want me to end, please show me clearly and give me the strength to obey you. Help me to walk in victory, with my life exhibiting the fruits of the Holy Spirit. I want your purposes to be fulfilled in me. Amen.

PRAYER

Lord, help me to be content right where you have me. Help me to walk in your ways and be willing to wait for your timing in everything I undertake. If a mate is in your plan for me, send that one you have created just for me. If not, may I know that whatever you have planned for me is better than what I could design.

19

Material Provision

JOB LAY-OFF... BANKRUPTCIES... BUY-OUTS... plant closings... shortages of affordable housing... rising mortgage rates... soaring living costs. The trigger of economic pressure can ignite alienation in families, marital strife, addictions, anger, even riots.

Are Christians immune to these realities which pervade our society? Not at all. Financial difficulties can easily strike fear into the heart of anyone who loses sight of God's promise to provide. Normally self-sufficient believers can suddenly feel like a rudderless boat bobbing on a choppy sea of uncertainty. They can even career out of control and threaten to shipwreck on the rocks despair.

Should we blame the devil for such a crisis? Or is it our own fault? Where is God in all this? Our culture fosters the notion that we should find the culprit for our troubles and file a lawsuit. Passing the blame began with Adam, who blamed Eve for offering him forbidden fruit. She in turn blamed the serpent for deceiving her (Genesis 3:11-13).

Ever since, we've been blaming one another or the government or the devil for the trials we suffer. Jesus identified the one most responsible when he said: "The thief [Satan] comes only to steal and kill and destroy; I have come that they may have life, and have it to the full" (John 10:10).

Satan ultimately lurks behind the misfortunes that rob us of financial security. He is the source of all evil. And what does he do when hard times hit us personally? He uses the opportunity to malign God and his faithfulness, to kill our hope, and destroy our faith. In the midst of distress, Satan wants us to blame God, rather than turn and acknowledge him as our source of help.

But we do have a choice. We can buy into the temptation to blame God and others. Or we can take responsibility for our own actions and attitudes and seek forgiveness for those that are wrong. We can choose to agree with Jesus' declaration: "I have come that they may have life, and have it to the full."

The word translated "life" here means "life in all its manifestations... life in activity... resurrection life and eternal life...."[1] In other words, Jesus' purpose for coming to earth was to provide a way for us to live a meaningful life at every level and dimension—spiritual, physical, and emotional.

WHY DO WE SUFFER NEED?

God created Adam and Eve, placed them in the Garden of Eden, and made every provision for their care. They had no need to worry about anything! But when these ancestors of ours chose to disobey God's command, they brought a curse upon themselves and upon all humankind. "By the sweat of your brow you will eat your food," God declared (Genesis 3:19). When he thrust them out of the garden to fend for themselves, anxiety about the future became our legacy as well.

But in his great mercy, God made covenant promises to his people. In essence he agreed, "If you will obey my word and walk in my ways, I will prosper you and your descendants, and through them all the nations of the earth will be blessed" (see Genesis 22:15-18). The word prosper in Hebrew is *chashar*, from which the word kosher is derived. It means "to be correctly aligned with certain requirements."

The keys to enjoying God's provision are:

1. To obey his Word.
2. To keep our eyes and hearts focused on him, not just on his blessings.
3. To resist the enemy's emphasis on how negative the circumstances may appear.
4. To be concerned about the needs of others.

Jesus taught this foundational principle to his disciples: "Therefore I tell you, do not worry about your life, what you will eat or drink; or about your body, what you will wear. Is not life more important than food, and the body more important than clothes?... For the pagans run after all these things, and your heavenly Father knows that you need them. But seek first his kingdom and his righteousness, and all these things will be given to you as well" (Matthew 6:25, 32-33).

Believers who abide by the principle of tithing feel it is also a vital key to their having God's blessing of provision. The Scripture says:

> Will a man rob God? Yet you rob me.
> But you ask, "How do we rob you?"
> In tithes and offerings. You are under a curse—the whole nation of you—because you are robbing me. Bring the whole tithe into the storehouse, that there may be food in my house. Test me in this," says the LORD Almighty, "and see if I will not throw open the floodgates of heaven and pour out so much blessing that you will not have room enough for it. I will prevent pests from devouring your crops, and the vines in your fields will not cast their fruit," says the LORD Almighty. **Malachi 3:8-11**

Dr. Harold Lindsell says of this passage:

Malachi insists that failure to tithe is to rob God of what rightfully belongs to him. And as a result, the divine blessing is withheld from those who refuse to give God his due. Tithing is not commanded in the New Testament as a legal requirement, but the Christian under grace can hardly do less than the Jew under law. Tithing is the outward sign of an inward commitment that all one has belongs to God, who is entitled to a return on the divine investment in any individual.[2]

Believers who meet the requirement of obedience can still claim God's promises of blessing and provision today. But obedience also entails showing concern and generosity toward others. God punished the disobedience of Ananias and Sapphira by death, as recorded in Acts 5:1-11. Contrast his swift judgment of greed and selfishness with Paul's message in Philippians: "… for even when I was in Thessalonica, you sent me aid again and again when I was in need…. And my God will meet all your needs according to his glorious riches in Christ Jesus" (Philippians 4:16, 19).

You can "rebuke the devourer" by reminding him of God's abundant promise of provision in the following Scriptures.

SCRIPTURES

"Give, and it will be given to you. A good measure, pressed down, shaken together and running over, will be poured into your lap. For with the measure you use, it will be measured to you." Luke 6:38

Now he who supplies seed to the sower and bread for food will also supply and increase your store of seed and will enlarge the harvest of your righteousness. You will be made rich in every way so that you can be generous on every occasion,

and through us your generosity will result in thanksgiving to
God.   2 Corinthians 9:10-11

"If you follow my decrees and are careful to obey my commands, I will send you rain in its season, and the ground will
yield its crops and the trees of the field their fruit. Your
threshing will continue until grape harvest and the grape harvest will continue until planting, and you will eat all the food
you want and live in safety in your land.
    ... You will still be eating last year's harvest when you will
have to move it out to make room for the new...."
                                                        Leviticus 26:3-5, 10

Then Jesus declared, "I am the bread of life. He who comes to
me will never go hungry, and he who believes in me will never
be thirsty...." John 6:35

When you have eaten and are satisfied, praise the LORD your
God for the good land he has given you. Be careful that you
do not forget the LORD your God, failing to observe his commands, his laws and his decrees....
    ... for it is he who gives you the ability to produce wealth,
and so confirms his covenant, which he swore to your forefathers....   Deuteronomy 8:10-11, 18

So [Elijah] did what the LORD had told him. He went to the
Kerith Ravine, east of the Jordan, and stayed there. The
ravens brought him bread and meat in the morning and
bread and meat in the evening, and he drank from the brook.
    Some time later the brook dried up because there had
been no rain in the land. Then the word of the LORD came to
him: "Go at once to Zarephath of Sidon and stay there. I have
commanded a widow in that place to supply you with food."
                                                        1 Kings 17:5-9

Then the Spirit of God came upon Zechariah.... He stood
before the people and said, "This is what God says: 'Why do
you disobey the LORD's commands? You will not prosper.

Because you have forsaken the LORD, he has forsaken you.'"

2 Chronicles 24:20

Blessed is the man
   who does not walk in the counsel of the wicked
or stand in the way of sinners
   or sit in the seat of mockers.
But his delight is in the law of the LORD,
   and on his law he meditates day and night.
He is like a tree planted by streams of water,
   which yields its fruit in season
and whose leaf does not wither.
   Whatever he does prospers.   **Psalm 1:1-3**

The poor will eat and be satisfied;
   they who seek the LORD will praise him—
   may your hearts live forever!   **Psalm 22:26**

The LORD is my shepherd, I shall not be in want.
   He makes me lie down in green pastures,
he leads me beside quiet waters,
   he restores my soul.
He guides me in paths of righteousness
   for his name's sake.
Even though I walk
   through the valley of the shadow of death,
I will fear no evil,
   for you are with me;
your rod and your staff,
   they comfort me.
You prepare a table before me
   in the presence of my enemies.
You anoint my head with oil;
   my cup overflows.
Surely goodness and love will follow me
   all the days of my life,
and I will dwell in the house of the LORD
   forever.   **Psalm 23**

Praise to the Lord our savior,
   who daily bears our burdens.   **Psalm 68:19**

   ... the LORD bestows favor and honor;
no good thing does he withhold
   from those whose walk is blameless.   **Psalm 84:11**

He makes grass grow for the cattle,
   and plants for man to cultivate—
   bringing forth food from the earth:
wine that gladdens the heart of man,
   oil to make his face shine,
   and bread that sustains his heart.   **Psalm 104:14-15**

Great are the works of the LORD;
   they are pondered by all who delight in them....
He provides food for those who fear him;
   he remembers his covenant forever.   **Psalm 111:2, 5**

Trust in the LORD with all your heart
   and lean not on your own understanding;
in all your ways acknowledge him,
   and he will make your paths straight.

Do not be wise in your own eyes;
   fear the LORD and shun evil.
This will bring health to your body
   and nourishment to your bones.
Honor the LORD with your wealth,
   with the firstfruits of all your crops;
then your barns will be filled to overflowing,
   and your vats will brim over with new wine.   **Proverbs 3:5-10**

Blessed is the man who listens to me,
   watching daily at my doors,
   waiting at my doorway.
For whoever finds me finds life
   and receives favor from the LORD.   **Proverbs 8:34-35**

My people will live in peaceful dwelling places,
in secure homes,
in undisturbed places of rest.   **Isaiah 32:18**

"... Instead of the thornbush will grow the pine tree, and instead of briers the myrtle will grow.
This will be for the LORD's renown,
for an everlasting sign,
which will not be destroyed."   **Isaiah 55:13**

... if you spend yourselves in behalf of the hungry
and satisfy the needs of the oppressed,
then your light will rise in the darkness,
and your night will become like the noonday.
The LORD will guide you always;
he will satisfy your needs in a sun-scorched land
and will strengthen your frame.
You will be like a well-watered garden,
like a spring whose waters never fail.   **Isaiah 58:10-11**

The threshing floors will be filled with grain;
the vats will overflow with new wine and oil.
"I will repay you for the years the locusts have eaten...
You will have plenty to eat, until you are full,
and you will praise the name of the LORD your God,
who has worked wonders for you;
never again will my people be shamed."   **Joel 2:24-26**

"If you remain in me and my words remain in you, ask whatever you wish, and it will be given you."   **John 15:7**

He who did not spare his own Son, but gave him up for us all—how will he not also, along with him, graciously give us all things?   **Romans 8:32**

Not that we are competent in ourselves to claim anything for ourselves, but our competence comes from God.   **2 Corinthians 3:5**

For you know the grace of our Lord Jesus Christ, that though he was rich, yet for your sakes he became poor, so that you through his poverty might become rich. **2 Corinthians 8:9**

Remember this: Whoever sows sparingly will also reap sparingly, and whoever sows generously will also reap generously. Each man should give what he has decided in his heart to give, not reluctantly or under compulsion, for God loves a cheerful giver. And God is able to make all grace abound to you, so that in all things at all times, having all that you need, you will abound in every good work. **2 Corinthians 9:6-8**

... we brought nothing into the world, and we can take nothing out of it. But if we have food and clothing, we will be content with that. People who want to get rich fall into temptation and a trap and into many foolish and harmful desires that plunge men into ruin and destruction. For the love of money is a root of all kinds of evil. Some people, eager for money, have wandered from the faith and pierced themselves with many griefs. **1 Timothy 6:7-10**

Command those who are rich in this present world not to be arrogant nor to put their hope in wealth, which is so uncertain, but to put their hope in God, who richly provides us with everything for our enjoyment. Command them to do good, to be rich in good deeds, and to be generous and willing to share. In this way they will lay up treasure for themselves as a firm foundation for the coming age, so that they may take hold of the life that is truly life. **1 Timothy 6:17-19**

Let us then approach the throne of grace with confidence, so that we may receive mercy and find grace to help us in our time of need. **Hebrews 4:16**

Cast all your anxiety on him because he cares for you. **1 Peter 5:7**

A PRAYER FOR PROVISION

Father, thank you for the promises for provision in your Word. I acknowledge you as the source of everything I need for my spirit, soul, and body. Lord, help me to trust you for all my needs, but also help me to be generous in reaching out to the needs of others. Thank you that I can cast all my care and anxiety upon you, knowing you care for me—your child. Help me to walk in this new level of faith. I praise you for your faithfulness, in Jesus' name. Amen.

20

Protection and Security

"GOD IS OUR REFUGE AND STRENGTH, an ever-present help in trouble" (Psalm 46:1). When disaster—or even the fear of trouble—looms larger than life on our horizon, we need assurance of God's protection. When we search the Word of God for such reminders, we begin to feel more secure.

One helpful approach is to find in Scripture the story of someone's dilemma comparable to the one confronting you, then discover how the matter was resolved with the help of the Lord. Ask the Holy Spirit to guide your study. In the process you will often can find verses to use as ammunition in your spiritual warfare, as well as to keep yourself encouraged.

Psalm 91 offers dramatic assurance that God will protect and rescue his child in trouble:

He who dwells in the shelter of the Most High
  will rest in the shadow of the Almighty.
I will say of the LORD, "He is my refuge and my fortress,
  my God, in whom I trust."

Surely he will save you from the fowler's snare
  and from the deadly pestilence.
He will cover you with his feathers,
  and under his wings you will find refuge;
  his faithfulness will be your shield and rampart.
You will not fear the terror of night,
  nor the arrow that flies by day,
nor the pestilence that stalks in the darkness,
  nor the plague that destroys at midday.
A thousand may fall at your side,
  ten thousand at your right hand,
  but it will not come near you.
You will only observe with your eyes
  and see the punishment of the wicked.

If you make the Most High your dwelling—
  even the LORD, who is my refuge—
then no harm will befall you,
  no disaster will come near your tent.
For he will command his angels concerning you
  to guard you in all your ways;
they will lift you up in their hands,
  so that you will not strike your foot against a stone.
You will tread upon the lion and the cobra;
  you will trample the great lion and the serpent.

"Because he loves me," says the LORD, "I will rescue him;
  I will protect him, for he acknowledges my name.
He will call upon me, and I will answer him;
  I will be with him in trouble,
  I will deliver him and honor him.
With long life will I satisfy him
  and show him my salvation."

REMOVE DESECRATION

Notice that this promise has a condition attached. We must make the Most High our dwelling-place if we want his protection. One way of doing so is to honor him in our dwelling place by removing any desecration from our homes, offices, hotel rooms, etc. Tom White explains:

> Evil spirits can pollute places with their unholy presence. Such demonization usually occurs when mortal beings commit immoral acts that open the door to the activity of demons. For example, a house used for the manufacture or selling of drugs, a place used for prostitution, or a building used by a fortune-teller or spiritualist group may invite demons of bondage, deception, violence, lust, sexual perversion, or familiar spirits of the occult. Even when the perpetrators have left the scene, evil spirits may linger, hoping to prey upon unsuspecting newcomers.[1]

It is important to rid your home of any object that even hints of occult involvement or idol worship. Some Christians returning from trips abroad innocently bring back artifacts such as fetishes, face masks, "sacred" writings, carved figures of gods, etc. which have been "prayed" over by heathen priests or used in idol worship in some way.

God gave clear instructions in these matters: "The images of their gods you are to burn in the fire. Do not covet the silver and gold on them, and do not take it for yourselves, or you will be ensnared by it, for it is detestable to the LORD your God. Do not bring a detestable thing into your house.... Utterly abhor and detest it, for it is set apart for destruction" (Deuteronomy 7:25-26).

Josiah, a king of Judah, offers a biblical example of obedience in the matter: "Furthermore, Josiah got rid of the mediums and spiritists, the household gods, the idols and all the other detestable things seen in Judah and Jerusalem. This he did to fulfill the requirements of the law written in the book

196 / The Spiritual Warrior's Prayer Guide

that Hilkiah the priest had discovered in the temple of the LORD" (2 Kings 23:24).

When Paul evangelized in Ephesus, the new converts wasted no time in cleaning house: "A number who had practiced sorcery brought their scrolls together and burned them publicly. When they calculated the value of the scrolls, the total came to fifty thousand drachmas" (Acts 19:19).

The following Scriptures can prove helpful as you build your faith in God's protection and security, no matter how vulnerable your present situation may seem. Remember to speak the Word aloud. Our proclamation of the truth is heard by a vast invisible world—God and his angels, as well as Satan and his demonic hosts. We invoke God's protection to shield us from enemy assaults. We strengthen our own faith as we hear ourselves affirm the truth of God.

SCRIPTURES

I will lie down and sleep in peace,
   for you alone, O LORD,
   make me dwell in safety.   **Psalm 4:8**

For in the day of trouble
   he will keep me safe in his dwelling;
he will hide me in the shelter of his tabernacle
   and set me high upon a rock.   **Psalm 27:5**

The LORD is my strength and my shield;
   my heart trusts in him, and I am helped.
My heart leaps for joy
   and I will give thanks to him in song.   **Psalm 28:7**

The LORD gives strength to his people;
   the LORD blesses his people with peace.   **Psalm 29:11**

The salvation of the righteous comes from the LORD;
   he is their stronghold in time of trouble.   **Psalm 37:39**

But I will sing of your strength,
  in the morning I will sing of your love;
for you are my fortress,
  my refuge in times of trouble.   **Psalm 59:16**

Those who trust in the LORD are like Mount Zion,
  which cannot be shaken but endures forever.
As the mountains surround Jerusalem,
  so the LORD surrounds his people
  both now and forevermore.
The scepter of the wicked will not remain
  over the land allotted to the righteous,
for then the righteous might use
  their hands to do evil.   **Psalm 125:1-3**

Praise be to the LORD my Rock,
  who trains my hands for war,
  my fingers for battle.
He is my loving God and my fortress,
  my stronghold and my deliverer,
my shield, in whom I take refuge,
  who subdues peoples under me.   **Psalm 144:1-2**

Oh LORD, you have searched me
  and you know me....
You discern my going out and my lying down;
  you are familiar with all my ways....

You hem me in—behind and before;
  you have laid your hand upon me.
Such knowledge is too wonderful for me,
  too lofty for me to attain.   **Psalm 139:1, 3, 5-6**

Rescue me, O LORD, from evil men;
  protect me from men of violence,
who devise evil plans in their hearts
  and stir up war every day.

They make their tongues as sharp as a serpent's;
    the poison of vipers is on their lips.

Keep me, O LORD, from the hands of the wicked;
  protect me from men of violence
    who plan to trip my feet.
Proud men have hidden a snare for me;
    they have spread out the cords of their net
    and have set traps for me along my path.

O LORD, I say to you, "You are my God."
    Hear O LORD, my cry for mercy.
O Sovereign LORD, my strong deliverer,
    who shields my head in the day of battle—
do not grant the wicked their desires, O LORD;
    do not let their plans succeed.... **Psalm 140:1-8**

The LORD watches over you—
    the LORD is your shade at your right hand;
the sun will not harm you by day,
    nor the moon by night.

The LORD will keep you from all harm—
    he will watch over your life;
the LORD will watch over your coming and going
    both now and forevermore. **Psalm 121:5-8**

Even in darkness light dawns for the upright,
    for the gracious and compassionate and righteous man.
Psalm 112:4

The LORD's curse is on the house of the wicked,
but he blesses the home of the righteous. **Proverbs 3:33**

"The fear of the LORD is the beginning of wisdom,
    and knowledge of the Holy One is understanding.
For through me your days will be many,
    and years will be added to your life." **Proverbs 9:10-11**

You have been a refuge for the poor,
    a refuge for the needy in his distress,
a shelter from the storm
    and a shade from the heat.
For the breath of the ruthless
    is like a storm driving against a wall
    and like the heat of the desert.
You silence the uproar of foreigners;
    as heat is reduced by the shadow of a cloud,
    so the song of the ruthless is stilled.   **Isaiah 25:4-5**

Even to your old age and gray hairs
    I am he, I am he who will sustain you.
I have made you and I will carry you;
    I will sustain you and I will rescue you.   **Isaiah 46:4**

The LORD is good,
    a refuge in times of trouble.
He cares for those who trust in him...   **Nahum 1:7**

God is just: He will pay back trouble to those who trouble you and give relief to you who are troubled, and to us as well. This will happen when the Lord Jesus is revealed from heaven in blazing fire with his powerful angels.   **2 Thessalonians 1:6-7**

But the Lord is faithful, and he will strengthen and protect you from the evil one.   **2 Thessalonians 3:3**

We know that anyone born of God does not continue to sin; the one who was born of God keeps him safe, and the evil one cannot harm him.   **1 John 5:18**

The Lord will rescue me from every evil attack and will bring me safely to his heavenly kingdom. To him be glory for ever and ever. Amen.   **2 Timothy 4:18**

SCRIPTURES ON GOD AS OUR SHIELD

"Blessed are you, O Israel!
  Who is like you,
  a people saved by the LORD?
He is your shield and helper
  and your glorious sword.
Your enemies will cower before you,
  and you will trample down their high places."
  Deuteronomy 33:29

My God is my rock, in whom I take refuge,
  my shield and the horn of my salvation.
He is my stronghold, my refuge and my savior—
  from violent men you save me.   **2 Samuel 22:3**

"As for God, his way is perfect;
  the word of the LORD is flawless.
He is a shield
  for all who take refuge in him."   **2 Samuel 22:31**

For surely, O LORD, you bless the righteous;
  you surround them with your favor as with a shield.
  Psalm 5:12

You give me your shield of victory,
  and your right hand sustains me;
  you stoop down to make me great.   **Psalm 18:35**

You are my refuge and my shield;
  I have put my hope in your word.   **Psalm 119:114**

He is my loving God and my fortress,
  my stronghold and my deliverer,
my shield, in whom I take refuge,
  who subdues peoples under me.   **Psalm 144:2**

A PRAYER FOR PROTECTION

Lord, may I always dwell in your shelter, for you are my refuge and my fortress. You are my God. I trust in you. You will answer me when I am in trouble and deliver me. Thank you that you are a shield round about me. Whenever I am afraid you are there watching over me. Thank you for your protection and security. I pray in the name of Jesus Christ, my Savior. Amen.

PART FOUR

Standing in the Gap

21

Healing

S ICKNESS, ALONG WITH SIN AND SEPARATION FROM GOD, is a
painful result of man's rebellion against God. That first
sin in the garden destroyed human innocence and opened a
veritable floodgate, allowing rivers of sin to wash over the
human race. Sickness, pain, and death also came crashing
through that gate.

We inherit from Adam and Eve both our inclination to sin
and our vulnerability to sickness and disease. But God provided a solution by sending his Son as the perfect sacrifice for
sin. His perfect provision for sin also includes healing of soul,
mind, and body. Speaking of Jesus, Isaiah prophesied:

Surely he took up our infirmities
    and carried our sorrows,
yet we considered him stricken by God,
    smitten by him, and afflicted.
But he was pierced for our transgressions,
    he was crushed for our iniquities;
the punishment that brought us peace was upon him,
    and by his wounds we are healed. **Isaiah 53:4-5**

Divine health is God's best for us. But many factors—some our own fault, some because we are members of a fallen race, some the work of the enemy—frustrate God's plan. His higher plan, however, is to conform us to the image of his Son (see Romans 8:29).

Healing was clearly important to Jesus. He not only healed the sick himself, he commissioned his followers to do the same: "When Jesus had called the Twelve together, he gave them power and authority to drive out all demons and to cure diseases, and he sent them out to preach the kingdom of God and to heal the sick" (Luke 9:1-2).

God's power to heal has not diminished one bit today. And he continues to search for disciples who will pray for the sick. God touches sick bodies with his healing power every day. Sometimes our prayer and spiritual warfare is coupled with modern medical technology. Other times we see instant miracles. Or in some cases, prayer may help to accelerate the body's efforts to heal itself.

OUR PRIVILEGE OF PRAYER

Our privilege is to pray for healing, and God's prerogative is to heal in his own way and timing. We cooperate with him by reminding ourselves and the devil of God's promise of healing through the blood of Jesus Christ. But we must guard against insisting on our own "formula" of exactly how and when God will heal.

Sometimes our prayers for healing may prolong a person's life, yet we don't see the total healing for which we had hoped. Such an outcome does not necessarily mean defeat. We must recognize that prayer and spiritual warfare can extend life to allow people time to "get their house in order" —both in spiritual and in practical matters—or time to accomplish a particular task or goal in life which God intends them to do.

As spiritual warriors, we should focus our attention on Jesus —to worship, love, and know him in an intimate way, even in the midst of pain and distress. Ask for wisdom and discernment as to how to pray for a needed healing, then engage in prayer and spiritual warfare and trust the Lord to intervene in miraculous ways.

DISOBEDIENCE IS DEADLY

It is unreasonable to habitually disobey God's natural and spiritual laws, yet expect him to keep us well. Recognizing that our body is the temple of the Holy Spirit, we should use good sense in not abusing it with harmful substances or foods that lack nutrition.

Disobedience and sin can bring on the consequences of sickness in our bodies. When Miriam began to talk against her brother Moses, the anger of the Lord came against her; she was stricken with leprosy (see Numbers 12:9-10). King Jehoram sinned, then the Lord afflicted him with an incurable disease of the bowels and he soon died (see 2 Chronicles 21:18-19).

Of course, we must not assume that just because someone has a sickness, they have necessarily sinned—or that they lack faith to believe God for healing. We should pray—and encourage them to pray—for an understanding of the cause of the illness and direction on how to pray.

Dean Sherman reminds us that sickness can have other reasons besides being caused by the devil:

Sickness can be caused by germs. Most often we are sick, not because of the devil, nor because of sin in our lives, nor because of the judgment from God. We are sick from bacteria, viruses, or physiological abnormalities. This is the world in which we live. We may be sick because of inherent weaknesses.

... Sickness can also be the result of abuse to our bodies. Improper diet, lack of exercise, or lack of rest may bring illness.[1]

SAMPLE SCRIPTURAL WARFARE

First forgive anyone against whom you hold any grudge or complaint. Confess any known sin. Ask God to forgive you, then receive and accept his forgiveness. Next, address the enemy aloud in words like these:

I declare to the powers of darkness in the heavenly realms, I come against this sickness in the name of the Lord Jesus Christ of Nazareth. It is written in God's Word that the one [Jesus] who is in me is greater than the one [Satan] who is in the world (1 John 4:4). I declare this attack null and void. Because I draw near to God and resist you, devil, you have to flee according to James 4:7.

Now begin to praise and worship God, exalting him as your healer. Read aloud some of the psalms in praise of him. For example:

I will extol the LORD at all times;
   his praise will always be on my lips.
My soul will boast in the LORD;
   let the afflicted hear and rejoice.
Glorify the LORD with me;
   let us exalt his name together.

I sought the LORD, and he answered me;
   he delivered me from all my fears. **Psalm 34:1-4**

SCRIPTURES ON HEALING

Don't you know that you yourselves are God's temple and that God's Spirit lives in you? If anyone destroys God's temple,

God will destroy him; for God's temple is sacred, and you are that temple. 1 Corinthians 3:16-17

And without faith it is impossible to please God, because anyone who comes to him must believe that he exists and that he rewards those who earnestly seek him. Hebrews 11:6

O LORD my God, I called to you for help
  and you healed me.
O LORD, you brought me up from the grave;
  you spared me from going down into the pit.

Sing to the LORD, you saints of his;
  praise his holy name. Psalm 30:2-3

... who forgives all your sins
  and heals all your diseases,
who redeems your life from the pit
  and crowns you with love and compassion.... Psalm 103:3-4

Turn to me and be gracious to me,
  for I am lonely and afflicted.
The troubles of my heart have multiplied;
  free me from my anguish.
Look upon my affliction and my distress
  and take away all my sins. Psalm 25:16-18

Then they cried to the LORD in their trouble,
  and he saved them from their distress.
He sent forth his word and healed them;
  he rescued them from the grave. Psalm 107:19-20

The LORD upholds all those who fall
  and lifts up all who are bowed down....
The LORD is near to all who call on him, to all who
  call on him in truth. Psalm 145:14, 18

... The LORD gives sight to the blind,
the LORD lifts up those who are bowed down,
   the LORD loves the righteous.   **Psalm 146:8**

Do not be wise in your own eyes;
   fear the LORD and shun evil.
This will bring health to your body
   and nourishment to your bones.   **Proverbs 3:7-8**

A cheerful heart is good medicine,
   but a crushed spirit dries up the bones.   **Proverbs 17:22**

My son, pay attention to what I say;
   listen closely to my words.
Do not let them out of your sight,
   keep them within your heart;
for they are life to those who find them
   and health to a man's whole body.   **Proverbs 4:20-21**

Heal me, O LORD, and I will be healed;
   save me and I will be saved,
   for you are the one I praise.   **Jeremiah 17:14**

"But I will restore you to health
   and heal your wounds,"
      declares the LORD....   **Jeremiah 30:17**

Jesus went throughout Galilee, teaching in their synagogues, preaching the good news of the kingdom, and healing every disease and sickness among the people.   **Matthew 4:23**

When he had gone indoors, the blind men came to him, and he asked them, "Do you believe that I am able to do this?"
   "Yes, Lord," they replied.
   Then he touched their eyes and said, "According to your faith will it be done to you;" and their sight was restored.
Matthew 9:28-29

Great crowds came to [Jesus], bringing the lame, the blind, the crippled, the mute and many others, and laid them at his feet; and he healed them. The people were amazed when they saw the mute speaking, the crippled made well, the lame walking and the blind seeing. And they praised the God of Israel.   **Matthew 15:30-31**

Just then a woman who had been subject to bleeding for twelve years came up behind [Jesus] and touched the edge of his cloak. She said to herself, "If I only touch his cloak, I will be healed."

Jesus turned and saw her. "Take heart, daughter," he said, "your faith has healed you." And the woman was healed from that moment.   **Matthew 9:20-22**

When Jesus entered the ruler's house and saw the flute players and the noisy crowd, he said, "Go away. The girl is not dead but asleep." But they laughed at him. After the crowd had been put outside, he went in and took the girl by the hand, and she got up. News of this spread through all that region.   **Matthew 9:23-26**

[Jesus] welcomed them and spoke to them about the kingdom of God, and healed those who needed healing.   **Luke 9:11**

"And these signs will accompany those who believe: In my name [the name of Jesus] they will drive out demons;... they will place their hands on sick people, and they will get well."

Mark 16:17-18

These twelve Jesus sent out with the following instructions:... "Heal the sick, raise the dead, cleanse those who have leprosy, drive out demons. Freely you have received, freely give."

Matthew 10:5, 8

"Have faith in God," Jesus answered. "I tell you the truth, if anyone says to this mountain, 'Go throw yourself into the sea,' and does not doubt in his heart but believes that what he says will happen, it will be done for him. Therefore I tell you, whatever you ask for in prayer, believe that you have received it, and it will be yours. And when you stand praying, if you hold anything against anyone, forgive him, so that your Father in heaven may forgive you your sins." **Mark 11:22-25**

Now a man crippled from birth was being carried to the temple gate called Beautiful, where he was put every day to beg from those going into the temple courts. When he saw Peter and John about to enter, he asked them for money. Peter looked straight at him, as did John. Then Peter said, "Look at us!" So the man gave them his attention, expecting to get something from them.

Then Peter said, "Silver or gold I do not have, but what I have I give you. In the name of Jesus Christ of Nazareth, walk." Taking him by the right hand, he helped him up, and instantly the man's feet and ankles became strong. He jumped to his feet and began to walk. Then he went with them into the temple courts, walking and jumping, and praising God.

Acts 3:2-8

The apostles performed many miraculous signs and wonders among the people.... More and more men and women believed in the Lord and were added to their number. As a result, people brought the sick into the streets and laid them on beds and mats so that at least Peter's shadow might fall on some of them as he passed by. Crowds gathered also from the towns around Jerusalem, bringing their sick and those tormented by evil spirits, and all of them were healed. **Acts 5:12-16**

In Lystra there sat a man crippled in his feet, who was lame from birth and had never walked. He listened to Paul as he was speaking. Paul looked directly at him, saw that he had faith to be healed and called out, "Stand up on your feet!" At that, the man jumped up and began to walk. **Acts 14:8-10**

God did extraordinary miracles through Paul, so that even handkerchiefs and aprons that had touched him were taken to the sick, and their illnesses were cured and the evil spirits left them.   Acts 19:11-12

Is any one of you sick? He should call the elders of the church to pray over him and anoint him with oil in the name of the Lord. And the prayer offered in faith will make the sick person well; the Lord will raise him up. If he has sinned, he will be forgiven. Therefore confess your sins to each other and pray for each other so that you may be healed. The prayer of a righteous man is powerful and effective.   James 5:14-16

He himself bore our sins in his body on the tree, so that we might die to sins and live for righteousness; by his wounds you have been healed. 1 Peter 2:24

Dear friend, I pray that you may enjoy good health and that all may go well with you, even as your soul is getting along well.   3 John 2

AN INTERCESSORY PRAYER FOR HEALING

In the name of Jesus Christ, by the authority of his shed blood, we come against every plot of Satan against [person's name] body. We thank you, Lord, that your Word energizes and gives life, and that you are giving that life to our brother/sister as we pray.

Father, bring healing and wholeness to the tissue, joints, marrow and fiber, to the blood system, and to the other systems of the body affected by this illness. May the medications he/she is taking have a beneficial effect, and all negative side effects be nullified in Jesus' name. Lord, cause his/her body to function as you created it to function.

We annihilate the enemy's plan of destruction. We cover

[person's name] with the blood of Jesus. We ask you to strengthen him/her with might in the inner man. We call upon the life that is in Jesus Christ to cause the enemy to flee. We thank you for victory, in Jesus' name. Amen.

22

Deliverance

E VER SINCE THE ARCHANGEL LUCIFER and his cohorts were cast out of heaven, they have been oppressing the human race. Lucifer was renamed Satan, meaning "adversary." We readily see evidence of his destructive work in our own lives, the lives of our loved ones, and in the nations of the world.

E.M. Bounds states:

> … Satan sows the tares in the wheat… bad thoughts among good thoughts. All kinds of evil seed are sown by him in the harvest fields of earth. He is always trying to make the good bad and the bad worse. He fills the mind of Judas, and he inflames and hurries him on to his infamous purpose…. The devil goes about as fierce, as resolute, and as strong as a lion, intent only to destroy.[1]

BREAKING BONDAGES

The good news of the gospel is that Christ came to destroy the devil's work (1 John 3:8). And he told his followers, "I have given you authority... to overcome all the power of the enemy..." (Luke 10:19). The word "all" here signifies the totality, every level of power.

So why do we still see believers struggling against various bondages? Because somewhere they've left a door open that allows the enemy access to their lives. Some of the primary causes are unforgiveness, immorality, occult involvement, substance abuse, disobeying God's Word, rebelling against spiritual authority, and spiritual pride.

Here are three key scriptural warnings:

> Let no one be found among you who sacrifices his son or daughter in the fire, who practices divination or sorcery, interprets omens, engages in witchcraft, or casts spells, or who is a medium or spiritist or who consults the dead.... You must be blameless before the LORD your God.
>
> **Deuteronomy 18:10-13**

> "In your anger do not sin": Do not let the sun go down while you are still angry, and do not give the devil a foothold. **Ephesians 4:26-27**

> If you forgive anyone, I also forgive him. And what I have forgiven—if there was anything to forgive—I have forgiven in the sight of Christ for your sake, in order that Satan might not outwit us. For we are not unaware of his schemes.
>
> **2 Corinthians 2:10-11**

Many people fail to take such scriptural warnings seriously, thus opening themselves to Satan's dark kingdom when they disobey God's written commands. If the enemy has a foothold in your life, ask the Holy Spirit to reveal to you how he gained access. You may need to seek ministry and counsel from a minister or prayer partner as you deal with those specific areas.

If you are praying for an individual who needs deliverance, it is important to ask the Holy Spirit for revelation concerning the root cause of the problem. If you deal only with the symptom—the outward behavior—without getting to the root of the matter, the problem will only recur.

Study biblical examples of the devil's tactics. Remember that Satan is only a fallen archangel; never see him as an equal with God. To paint a clearer picture of the enemy's domain, Dean Sherman describes who inhabits the kingdom of darkness:

> ... Satan (an individual fallen archangel) and fallen angels, numerous demons, and evil spirits. According to God's Word, that is all there is. These spirits are personalities.... Jesus didn't confront a force of evil. He confronted evil spirits, sometimes naming them by name.
>
> ... Like all personalities, fallen angels think, listen, communicate, experience, act, and react. They speak to us in our minds.... They hear what we say, watch our reactions, and make plans and strategies.
>
> Because these evil personalities listen, we need to speak to them when we do spiritual warfare... rebuking them and verbally denying them access to our lives. Jesus addressed the enemy directly. Having told us that we would do greater things than he, Jesus has shown us by example that we too should address the enemy, resisting him.[2]

BINDING THE ENEMY

As intercessors we stand between God and a person, asking God to intervene for his or her need. But we also stand between Satan and that person, battling and pushing back the powers of darkness. To bind evil spirits means to restrain them by speaking directly to them and forbidding them to continue their destructive activity. The Holy Spirit's power energizes our words to loose the person from the enemy's hold. Then in prayer we ask the Holy Spirit to minister to that person's need and help him or her walk in obedience to God's Word.

Jesus himself provides a model for dealing boldly and authoritatively with demonic powers: "But if I drive out demons by the Spirit of God, then the kingdom of God has come upon you.... How can anyone enter a strong man's house and carry off his possessions unless he first ties up the strong man? Then he can rob his house" (Matthew 12:28-29). Jesus also told his followers: "I will give you the keys of the kingdom of heaven; whatever you bind on earth will be bound in heaven, and whatever you loose on earth will be loosed in heaven" (Matthew 16:19).

LEVELS OF WARFARE

Dr. C. Peter Wagner, in his book *Warfare Prayer*, suggests three generalized levels of spiritual warfare:

1. Ground level spiritual warfare... as when Jesus gave his disciples "power over unclean spirits, to cast them out..." (Matthew 10:1 NKJ).
2. Occult-level spiritual warfare... [involving] demonic power at work through shamans, New Age channelers, occult practitioners, witches and warlocks, satanist priests, fortune-tellers, and the like... (i.e. Paul's experience in Philippi as recorded in Acts 16:16-24).
3. Strategic-level spiritual warfare... [where] we contend with an even more ominous concentration of demonic power: territorial spirits. Paul writes that "we do not wrestle against flesh and blood, but against principalities, against powers, against the rulers of the darkness of this age, against spiritual hosts of wickedness in heavenly places" (Ephesians 6:12 NKJ).[3]

EXAMPLES IN JESUS' MINISTRY

Seven gospel stories illustrate our Lord's deliverance ministry:

The synagogue demoniac (Mark 1:21-28)
The Gerasene demoniac (Mark 5:1-20)
The Syrophoenician woman's daughter (Mark 7:24-30)
The epileptic boy (Mark 9:14-29)
The dumb demoniac (Matthew 9:32-34)
The blind/dumb demoniac (Matthew 12:22-24)
The woman bent with a spirit of infirmity (Luke 13:10-17)

... a man in their synagogue who was possessed by an evil spirit cried out, "What do you want with us, Jesus of Nazareth? Have you come to destroy us? I know who you are—the Holy One of God!"

"Be quiet!" said Jesus sternly. "Come out of him!" Mark 1:23-25

... a woman whose little daughter was possessed by an evil spirit came and fell at his feet.... She begged Jesus to drive the demon out of her daughter.

"First let the children eat all they want," he told her, "for it is not right to take the children's bread and toss it to their dogs."

"Yes, Lord," she replied, "but even the dogs under the table eat the children's crumbs."

Then he told her, "For such a reply, you may go; the demon has left your daughter."

She went home and found her child lying on the bed, and the demon gone. Mark 7:25-30

A man in the crowd answered, "Teacher, I brought you my son, who is possessed by a spirit that has robbed him of speech.... I asked your disciples to drive out the spirit, but they could not."

... [Jesus] rebuked the evil spirit. "You deaf and mute spirit," he said, "I command you, come out of him and never enter him again."

The spirit shrieked, convulsed him violently and came out.

... After Jesus had gone indoors, his disciples asked him privately, "Why couldn't we drive it out?"

He replied, "This kind can come out only by prayer."

Mark 9:17-29

While they were going out, a man who was demon-possessed and could not talk was brought to Jesus. And when the demon was driven out, the man who had been mute spoke. The crowd was amazed and said, "Nothing like this has ever been seen in Israel." **Matthew 9:32-33**

On a Sabbath Jesus was teaching in one of the synagogues, and a woman was there who had been crippled by a spirit for eighteen years. She was bent over and could not straighten up at all. When Jesus saw her, he called her forward and said to her, "Woman, you are set free from your infirmity." Then he put his hands on her, and immediately she straightened up and praised God....

The Lord answered him, "... should not this woman, a daughter of Abraham, whom Satan has kept bound for eighteen long years, be set free on the Sabbath day from what bound her?" **Luke 13:10-13, 15-16**

News about [Jesus] spread all over Syria, and people brought to him all who were ill with various diseases, those suffering severe pain, the demon-possessed, those having seizures, and the paralyzed, and he healed them. **Matthew 4:24**

When evening came, many who were demon-possessed were brought to him, and he drove out the spirits with a word and healed all the sick. **Matthew 8:16**

Moreover, demons came out of many people, shouting, "You are the Son of God!" but he rebuked them and would not allow them to speak, because they knew he was the Christ.

Luke 4:41

After this, Jesus traveled about from one town and village to another, proclaiming the good news of the kingdom of God. The Twelve were with him, and also some women who had been cured of evil spirits and diseases: Mary (called Magdalene) from whom seven demons had come out.... Luke 8:1-2

When Jesus had called the Twelve together, he gave them power and authority to drive out all demons and to cure diseases, and he sent them out to preach the kingdom of God and to heal the sick. Luke 9:1-2

"So if the Son sets you free, you will be free indeed." John 8:36

You know what has happened throughout Judea, beginning in Galilee after the baptism that John preached—how God anointed Jesus of Nazareth with the Holy Spirit and power, and how he went around doing good and healing all who were under the power of the devil, because God was with him.

Acts 10:37-38

DELIVERANCE IN THE APOSTLES' MINISTRY

Once when we were going to the place of prayer, we were met by a slave girl who had a spirit by which she predicted the future. She earned a great deal of money for her owners by fortune-telling. This girl followed Paul and the rest of us, shouting, "These men are servants of the Most High God, who are telling you the way to be saved." She kept this up for many days. Finally Paul became so troubled that he turned around and said to the spirit, "In the name of Jesus Christ I command you to come out of her!" At that moment the spirit left her. Acts 16:16-18

He has delivered us from such a deadly peril, and he will deliver us. On him we have set our hope that he will continue to deliver us.... 2 Corinthians 1:10

Dear friends, do not believe every spirit, but test the spirits to see whether they are from God, because many false prophets have gone out into the world. This is how you can recognize the Spirit of God: Every spirit that acknowledges that Jesus Christ has come in the flesh is from God, but every spirit that does not acknowledge Jesus is not from God. This is the spirit of the antichrist, which you have heard is coming and even now is already in the world.   1 John 4:1-3

A PRAYER FOR DELIVERANCE

Father, just as Jesus prayed that you would protect his disciples from the evil one, we ask that you also protect us by the power of his name. Reveal to us any area of our lives where we have allowed the enemy access. Give us your strategy to defeat the schemes and devices the devil tries to use against us. We need your battle plan to come against his attacks. May we be fully armed to fight for ourselves and our loved ones.

Thank you for the Holy Spirit who empowers us. Thank you for Jesus' shed blood on the cross that bought our deliverance at so great a price. Thank you that we can overcome by the blood of the Lamb, the Word of God, and our testimony. We rejoice in your victory! Amen.

23

Intercession
for Others

"WITHOUT GOD, WE CANNOT. Without us, God will not."
St. Augustine's succinct statement sums up the twofold nature of intercession. God empowers us by the Holy Spirit to intercede for others' needs; without that empowerment our prayers would be empty words.

God also invests us with Christ's authority to restrain satanic forces that are blinding and hindering the person for whom we're praying. God could restrain those forces without us if he chose to. But he has equipped us and commissioned us to intercede by pushing back the enemy, thus allowing the Holy Spirit to bring conviction that leads to repentance.

Two Old Testament verses depict the need for an intercessor to do battle for sinful man: "... [God] was appalled that there was no one to intervene" (Isaiah 59:16); "I looked for a man among them who would build up the wall and stand before me in the gap on behalf of the land so I would not have to destroy it, but I found none..." (Ezekiel 22:30).

Of course Jesus ultimately filled that gap. He became the mediator between God and man by giving himself as a sacrifice for sin. But believers should also see themselves as intercessors: standing between God and the person(s) for whom we are praying, pleading for God to intervene. We also stand between Satan and that person, battling and pushing back the powers of darkness.

BIBLICAL MODELS OF INTERCESSION

Joshua's battle with the Amalekites is a vivid example of the power of intercession. While Joshua and Israel's army fought, Moses, Aaron, and Hur interceded. God gave them victory in battle, but it required the cooperation of the intercessors and an army of fighters:

> So Joshua fought the Amalekites as Moses had ordered, and Moses, Aaron and Hur went to the top of the hill. As long as Moses held up his hands, the Israelites were winning, but whenever he lowered his hands, the Amalekites were winning. When Moses' hands grew tired, they took a stone and put it under him and he sat on it. Aaron and Hur held his hands up—one on one side, one on the other —so that his hands remained steady till sunset. So Joshua overcame the Amalekite army with the sword. **Exodus 17:10-13**

The Hebrew root word for intercessor or intercession is *paga* (paw-GAH), meaning "to come between, to assail, to cause to entreat."[1] When an Israeli soldier hits the mark in target practice, he shouts "Paga!"—the modern Hebrew equivalent of "Bull's eye!" Effective intercessors learn to "hit the bull's eye" with accuracy in their warfare.

PREPARING FOR INTERCESSION

Doubt, disobedience, and unbelief cloud our spiritual vision, bring condemnation, and prevent us from praying with faith and boldness. Just as the priests would cleanse themselves before going into God's presence to represent the people, so we need to prepare ourselves for the ministry of intercession. Repentance and a renewed commitment to obey the Lord make us ready to "approach the throne of grace with confidence" (Hebrews 4:16), and to take an offensive stand against the enemy.

Both the psalmist David and the Apostle John emphasize this principle: "Create in me a pure heart, O God, / and renew a steadfast spirit within me" (Psalm 51:10); "Dear friends, if our hearts do not condemn us, we have confidence before God and receive from him anything we ask, because we obey his commands and do what pleases him" (1 John 3:21-22).

WHY STAND IN THE GAP?

Why is it that some people seem apparently closed to the gospel message? Indifferent to Jesus' sacrifice for their sins? The Bible offers some clues.

1. "The god of this age has blinded the minds of unbelievers, so that they cannot see the light of the gospel of the glory of Christ..." (2 Corinthians 4:4).
2. "... the trap of the devil, who has taken them captive to do his will" (2 Timothy 2:26).
3. "... worries of this life, the deceitfulness of wealth and the desires for other things come in and choke the word, making it unfruitful" (Mark 4:19).
4. Lack of harvesters in the field sharing the gospel message. "Ask the Lord of the harvest, therefore, to send out workers into his harvest field" (Matthew 9:38).

God's Word tells us what kind of prayers to pray, who to pray for, and why:

I urge, then, first of all, that requests, prayers, intercession and thanksgiving be made for everyone—for kings and all those in authority, that we may live peaceful and quiet lives in all godliness and holiness. This is good, and pleases God our Savior, who wants all men to be saved and to come to a knowledge of the truth. For there is one God and one mediator between God and men, the man Christ Jesus, who gave himself as a ransom for all men.... 1 Timothy 2:1-6

Therefore he is able to save completely those who come to God through him, because he always lives to intercede for them. Hebrews 7:25

For this reason Christ is the mediator of a new covenant, that those who are called may receive the promised eternal inheritance—now that he has died as a ransom to set them free from the sins committed under the first covenant.
Hebrews 9:15

When the prophet Jeremiah was shut up in prison, the Lord wanted to reveal to him things in the future. He instructed Jeremiah, "Call to me and I will answer you and tell you great and unsearchable things you do not know" (Jeremiah 33:3).

To "call" here means to cry out—in an attempt to get one's attention—or to proclaim. Dick Eastman explains this passage more thoroughly:

God promised Jeremiah that if he would call to Him, not only would He answer him, but He would reveal to him "great and mighty" things that could not otherwise be known. The word "mighty" is better rendered "isolated" or "inaccessible." The suggestion is that God would give Jeremiah "revelational insight," revealing things that otherwise would be inaccessible or isolated.

Such "revelational insight" always has been essential for a clear understanding of victorious spiritual warfare. One cannot pray effectively without insight into how to pray, as well as into what things God truly longs for us to seek after in prayer.[2]

INTERCESSION IS HARD WORK

Paul was continually reminding believers in the early church to remain faithful in prayer. In closing his letter to the church at Colossae, he mentions one of his coworkers who was a faithful and hard-working intercessor: "Epaphras, who is one of you and a servant of Christ Jesus, sends greetings. He is always wrestling in prayer for you, that you may stand firm in all the will of God, mature and fully assured. I vouch for him that he is working hard for you and for those at Laodicea and Hierapolis" (Colossians 4:12-13).

The enemy uses whatever devices he can to keep those for whom we pray from coming to the knowledge of truth and receiving Jesus as Lord. To see them delivered may literally require that we "wrestle in prayer" as Epaphras did. But we're not alone in this important task. The Father provides a helper —the Holy Spirit—to help us hit the target in our prayers.

THE HOLY SPIRIT TEACHES US HOW TO PRAY

Before Jesus left this earth he promised his followers, "I will ask the Father, and He will give you another Comforter (Counselor, Helper, Intercessor, Advocate, Strengthener, and Standby) that He may remain with you forever; the Spirit of Truth.... He will teach you all things" (John 14:16-17, 26 AMP).

The Holy Spirit, our helper, teaches us to pray and strengthens us for battle. He testifies of Jesus, guides, reveals, comforts, imparts joy, gives spiritual gifts, liberates, empowers for service, and intercedes for us.

Paul describes how the Holy Spirit prays through us: "In the same way, the Spirit helps us in our weakness. We do not know what we ought to pray for, but the Spirit himself intercedes for us with groans that words cannot express. And he who searches our hearts knows the mind of the Spirit, because the Spirit intercedes for the saints in accordance with God's will" (Romans 8:26-27).

Interceding according to the will of God is a key principle for successful prayer. Many people believe the Holy Spirit intercedes through us by praying in an unknown tongue. Bible teacher Judson Cornwall says, "Prayer is the most valuable use of tongues for it is 'speaking to God.'" He goes on to explain:

> ... The Holy Spirit is certainly not limited to the English language nor is He confined to modern languages. He has access to every language ever used by mankind, and He is very familiar with the language used in heaven. When deep intercession is needed, the Spirit often uses a language that is beyond the intellectual grasp of the speaker to bypass the censorship of his or her conscious mind, thereby enabling the Spirit to say what needs to be prayed without arguing with the faith level of the one through whom the intercession flows.[3]

This gift of unknown tongues is available to all born-again Christians, not just those who lived in the first century after Christ. As a child of God, all you need to do is ask (see Luke 11:11-13).

SCRIPTURES ON THE HOLY SPIRIT

"And these signs will accompany those who believe: In my name they will drive out demons; they will speak in new tongues...." **Mark 16:17**

" ... But you will receive power when the Holy Spirit comes on you; and you will be my witnesses in Jerusalem, and in all Judea and Samaria, and to the ends of the earth." **Acts 1:8**

After they prayed, the place where they were meeting was shaken. And they were all filled with the Holy Spirit and spoke the word of God boldly. **Acts 4:31**

When Paul placed his hands on them, the Holy Spirit came on them, and they spoke in tongues and prophesied. Acts 19:6

For anyone who speaks in a tongue does not speak to men but to God. 1 Corinthians 14:2

For if I pray in a tongue, my spirit prays, but my mind is unfruitful. So what shall I do? I will pray with my spirit, but I will also pray with my mind; I will sing with my spirit, but I will also sing with my mind. 1 Corinthians 14:14-15

We are witnesses of these things, and so is the Holy Spirit, whom God has given to those who obey him. Acts 5:32

... God anointed Jesus of Nazareth with the Holy Spirit and power, and... he went around doing good and healing all who were under the power of the devil, because God was with him. Acts 10:38

While Peter was still speaking these words, the Holy Spirit came on all who heard the message. The circumcised believers who had come with Peter were astonished that the gift of the Holy Spirit had been poured out even on the Gentiles.

Acts 10:44-45

Therefore I tell you that no one who is speaking by the Spirit of God says, "Jesus be cursed," and no one can say, "Jesus is Lord," except by the Holy Spirit. 1 Corinthians 12:3

... because our gospel came to you not simply with words, but also with power, with the Holy Spirit and with deep conviction. You know how we lived among you for your sake.

1 Thessalonians 1:5

Guard the good deposit that was entrusted to you—guard it with the help of the Holy Spirit who lives in us. 2 Timothy 1:14

But you, dear friends, build yourselves up in your most holy faith and pray in the Holy Spirit. Jude 20

SCRIPTURES ON INTERCESSION

"... when you pray, go into your room, close the door and pray to your Father, who is unseen. Then your Father, who sees what is done in secret, will reward you. And when you pray, do not keep on babbling like pagans, for they think they will be heard because of their many words. Do not be like them, for your Father knows what you need before you ask him." **Matthew 6:6-8**

Therefore, since we have a great high priest who has gone through the heavens, Jesus the Son of God, let us hold firmly to the faith we profess. For we do not have a high priest who is unable to sympathize with our weaknesses, but we have one who has been tempted in every way, just as we are—yet was without sin. Let us then approach the throne of grace with confidence, so that we may receive mercy and find grace to help us in our time of need. **Hebrews 4:14-16**

Who may ascend the hill of the LORD?
Who may stand in his holy place?
He who has clean hands and a pure heart,
who does not lift up his soul to an idol
or swear by what is false.
He will receive blessing from the LORD
and vindication from God his Savior. **Psalm 24:3-5**

Come near to God and he will come near to you. Wash your hands, you sinners, and purify your hearts, you double-minded.... Therefore confess your sins to each other and pray for each other so that you may be healed. The prayer of a righteous man is powerful and effective. **James 4:8; 5:16**

A PRAYER FOR LOST LOVED ONES

Lord, thank you that it is not your will that my loved ones perish. Please send people across their path who can share the gospel message with power and conviction. God grant them repentance, leading to a personal relationship with Jesus.

I come against the forces of darkness which are blinding them and holding them back, in the name of Jesus Christ of Nazareth. Loose your hold on them so they will be free to accept Jesus as Savior and Lord. I tear down every stronghold of deception keeping them in the enemy's camp... [ask the Holy Spirit to reveal more specific strongholds you may need to address].

In Jesus' name and by his authority, these loved ones are coming out of the kingdom of darkness and into the kingdom of light. Lord, please reveal to them how much you love them. Overwhelm them with your grace that they may be saved. Thank you, Lord, that your plan and purpose for them will prevail. They will be saved! Amen.

24

Battling against Deception

S ATAN IS A MASTER OF DECEPTION, as we can observe in the following examples. First he deceived *himself* in heaven: "I will raise my throne/above the stars of God;/ I will sit enthroned on the mount of assembly..../ I will ascend above the tops of the clouds;/ I will make myself like the Most High" (Isaiah 14:13-14).

Then he deceived *Eve* in the garden: "You will not surely die.... when you eat of it your eyes will be opened, and you will be like God..." (Genesis 3:4-5).

He tried to deceive *Jesus* in the wilderness: "The devil led him up to a high place and showed him in an instant all the kingdoms of the world. And he said to him, '... So if you worship me, it will all be yours'" (Luke 4:5-7).

He succeeded in deceiving *Judas* in the upper room: "The evening meal was being served, and the devil had already prompted Judas... to betray Jesus.... As soon as Judas took the bread, Satan entered into him" (John 13:2, 27).

Jesus' prayer prevented him from succeeding with *Peter:* "... Simon, Satan has asked to sift you as wheat. But I have prayed for you, Simon, that your faith may not fail... (Luke 22:31-32).

Are we susceptible as well? You bet we are.

EASY PREY FOR DECEPTION

Because of our predisposition to sin with which we are born, all of us are easy prey for deception if our spiritual armor is not firmly in place. We can be deceived by the devil or his emissaries. We can be deceived by the seduction and smooth talk of others. We can be deceived by our our own pride, selfishness, and greed.

God continually warned his people against being deceived into worshiping the false gods of surrounding nations:

> Be careful, or you will be enticed to turn away and worship other gods and bow down to them. Then the LORD's anger will burn against you.... **Deuteronomy 11:16-17**

> If your very own brother, or your son or daughter, or the wife you love, or your closest friend secretly entices you, saying, "Let us go and worship other gods,"... do not yield to him or listen to him.... **Deuteronomy 13:6-8**

To be deceived simply means to believe a lie instead of the truth. Deception always contains a grain of truth, barely enough to make it seem believable. But truth and error cannot mix, just as iron cannot mix with clay.

The fall of Adam and Eve presents a classic case of deception. Various translations of Genesis 3:1 refer to the serpent as being clever, crafty, subtle, and cunning. He is a master charlatan. Bible scholar E.W. Bullinger writes:

> ... The fall of man had to do solely with the Word of God, and is centered in the sin of believing Satan's lie instead of Jehovah's truth.

The temptation of "the first man Adam" began with the question "Hath God said?" The temptation of "the second man, the Lord from heaven" began with the similar question, "If Thou be the Son of God," when the voice of the Father had scarcely died away which said "This IS My beloved Son."

All turned on the truth of what Jehovah had said.

... Wherever the Word of God is called in question, there we see the trail of "that old serpent, which is the Devil, and Satan."[1]

We can almost feel Paul's pain when we read: "for Demas, because he loved this world, has deserted me..." (2 Timothy 4:10). Most of us have suffered the pain of seeing another believer whom we know and love fall into deception of one kind or another. Those in some position of responsibility are often a likely target: intercessors, elders and leaders in a congregation, Bible teachers, pastors, worship leaders, missionaries.

Some just lose their zeal for the Lord and become occasional pew-sitters who represent no threat to the kingdom of darkness. Others fall into immorality or false doctrine and become an active reproach to the body of Christ. A few actually forsake God completely and become servants of Satan.

How does deception happen? It all begins with entertaining Satan's suggestive question: "Did God really say?" A person can begin to doubt God's Word. Soon that individual begins to believe his or her case is different somehow, and to rationalize the sin. Some even believe if they do good works for God, he will excuse their sin. Once a person believes the first lie, a host of others can march in unchallenged. We must all heed Paul's warning: "... if you think you are standing firm, be careful that you don't fall!" (1 Corinthians 10:12).

OLD TESTAMENT SCRIPTURES

Now the serpent was more crafty than any of the wild animals the LORD God had made. He said to the woman, "Did God really say, 'You must not eat from any tree in the garden'?"

The woman said to the serpent, "We may eat fruit from the trees in the garden, but God did say, 'You must not eat fruit from the tree that is in the middle of the garden, and you must not touch it, or you will die.'"

"You will not surely die," the serpent said to the woman.

Genesis 3:1-4

Blessed is the man
    whose sin the LORD does not count against him
    and in whose spirit is no deceit. **Psalm 32:2**

Do not withhold your mercy from me, O LORD;
    may your love and your truth always protect me.   **Psalm 40:11**

Why do you boast of evil, you mighty man?
    Why do you boast all day long,
    you who are a disgrace in the eyes of God?
Your tongue plots destruction;
    it is like a sharpened razor,
    you who practice deceit.
You love evil rather than good,
    falsehood rather than speaking the truth.   **Psalm 52:1-3**

No one who practices deceit
    will dwell in my house;
no one who speaks falsely
    will stand in my presence. **Psalm 101:7**

A scoundrel and villain,
    who goes about with a corrupt mouth,
    who winks with his eye,
    signals with his feet
    and motions with his fingers,
    who plots evil with deceit in his heart—
    he always stirs up dissension. **Proverbs 6:12-14**

Truthful lips endure forever,
    but a lying tongue lasts only a moment.

There is deceit in the hearts of those who plot evil,
  but joy for those who promote peace. **Proverbs 12:19-20**

Like a coating of glaze over earthenware
  are fervent lips with an evil heart.
A malicious man disguises himself with his lips,
  but in his heart he harbors deceit.
Though his speech is charming, do not believe him,
  for seven abominations fill his heart. **Proverbs 26:23-25**

"... You live in the midst of deception;
  in their deceit they refuse to acknowledge me,"
    declares the LORD.
  Therefore this is what the LORD Almighty says:
  "See, I will refine and test them,
    for what else can I do
    because of the sin of my people?
  Their tongue is a deadly arrow;
    it speaks with deceit.
  With his mouth each speaks cordially to his neighbor,
    but in his heart he sets a trap for him.
  Should I not punish them for this?"
    declares the LORD.
  "Should I not avenge myself
    on such a nation as this?" **Jeremiah 9:6-9**

The idols speak deceit,
  diviners see visions that lie;
they tell dreams that are false,
  they give comfort in vain.
Therefore the people wander like sheep
  oppressed for lack of a shepherd. **Zechariah 10:2**

THE WARNINGS OF JESUS

During his teaching ministry, Jesus said more than eighty
times, "I tell you the truth...." He knew the truth would pro-

tect his followers from error. His strongest warning concerning the end time was to "be not deceived...."

"Watch out for false prophets. They come to you in sheep's clothing, but inwardly they are ferocious wolves. By their fruit you will recognize them.... A good tree cannot bear bad fruit, and a bad tree cannot bear good fruit...

"Not everyone who says to me, 'Lord, Lord,' will enter the kingdom of heaven, but only he who does the will of my Father who is in heaven." **Matthew 7:15-21**

"Watch out that no one deceives you. For many will come in my name, claiming, 'I am the Christ,' and will deceive many.... For false Christs and false prophets will appear and perform great signs and miracles to deceive even the elect—if that were possible." **Matthew 24:4-5, 24**

"Why do you call me, 'Lord, Lord,' and do not do what I say? I will show you what he is like who comes to me and hears my words and puts them into practice. He is like a man building a house, who dug down deep and laid the foundation on rock. When a flood came, the torrent struck that house but could not shake it, because it was well built." **Luke 6:46-48**

"Watch out that you are not deceived. For many will come in my name, claiming, 'I am he,' and 'The time is near.' Do not follow them." **Luke 21:8**

The Word became flesh and made his dwelling among us. We have seen his glory, the glory of the One and Only, who came from the Father, full of grace and truth.... The law was given through Moses; grace and truth came through Jesus Christ. **John 1:14, 17**

"... If you hold to my teaching, you are really my disciples. Then you will know the truth, and the truth will set you free." **John 8:31-32**

THE TEACHING OF THE APOSTLES

Although they claimed to be wise, they became fools and exchanged the glory of the immortal God for images....

They exchanged the truth of God for a lie, and worshiped and served created things rather than the Creator—who is forever praised. **Romans 1:22-25**

As it is written:
   "There is no one righteous, not even one...
   Their throats are open graves;
      their tongues practice deceit....
   There is no fear of God before their eyes." **Romans 3:10, 13, 18**

For sin, seizing the opportunity afforded by the commandment, deceived me, and through the commandment put me to death. **Romans 7:11**

I urge you, brothers, to watch out for those who cause divisions and put obstacles in your way that are contrary to the teaching you have learned. Keep away from them. For such people are not serving our Lord Christ, but their own appetites. By smooth talk and flattery they deceive the minds of naive people. **Romans 16:17-18**

Do you not know that the wicked will not inherit the kingdom of God? Do not be deceived: Neither the sexually immoral nor idolaters nor adulterers nor male prostitutes nor homosexual offenders nor thieves nor the greedy nor drunkards nor slanderers nor swindlers will inherit the kingdom of God.
1 Corinthians 6:9-10

... we have renounced secret and shameful ways; we do not use deception, nor do we distort the word of God.... The god of this age has blinded the minds of unbelievers, so that they cannot see the light of the gospel of the glory of Christ, who is the image of God. **2 Corinthians 4:2-4**

You who are trying to be justified by law have been alienated from Christ; you have fallen away from grace....

You were running a good race. Who cut in on you and kept you from obeying the truth?   Galatians 5:4, 7

Then [when we become mature] we will no longer be infants, tossed back and forth by the waves, and blown here and there by every wind of teaching and by the cunning and craftiness of men in their deceitful scheming....

Let no one deceive you with empty words, for because of such things God's wrath comes on those who are disobedient. Therefore do not be partners with them.   Ephesians 4:14; 5:6-7

See to it that no one takes you captive through hollow and deceptive philosophy, which depends on human tradition and the basic principles of this world rather than on Christ....

Therefore do not let anyone judge you by what you eat or drink, or with regard to a religious festival, a New Moon celebration or a Sabbath day. These are a shadow of the things that were to come; the reality, however, is found in Christ.
                                                Colossians 2:8, 16-17

The coming of the lawless one will be in accordance with the work of Satan displayed in all kinds of counterfeit miracles, signs and wonders, and in every sort of evil that deceives those who are perishing. They perish because they refused to love the truth and so be saved. For this reason God sends them a powerful delusion so that they will believe the lie....
                                                2 Thessalonians 2:9-11

If anyone teaches false doctrines and does not agree to the sound instruction of our Lord Jesus Christ and to godly teaching, he is conceited and understands nothing. He has an unhealthy interest in controversies and quarrels about words that result in envy, strife, malicious talk, evil suspicions and constant friction between men of corrupt mind, who have been robbed of the truth and who think that godliness is a means to financial gain.   1 Timothy 6:3-5

... evil men and impostors will go from bad to worse, deceiving and being deceived. But as for you, continue in what you have learned and have become convinced of, because you know those from whom you learned it, and how from infancy you have known the holy Scriptures, which are able to make you wise for salvation through faith in Christ Jesus.

2 Timothy 3:13-15

For the time will come when men will not put up with sound doctrine. Instead, to suit their own desires, they will gather around them a great number of teachers to say what their itching ears want to hear. They will turn their ears away from the truth and turn aside to myths. **2 Timothy 4:3-4**

At one time we too were foolish, disobedient, deceived and enslaved by all kinds of passions and pleasures.... But when the kindness and love of God our Savior appeared, he saved us... because of his mercy. **Titus 3:3-5**

If we deliberately keep on sinning after we have received the knowledge of the truth, no sacrifice for sins is left, but only a fearful expectation of judgment and of raging fire that will consume the enemies of God. **Hebrews 10:26-27**

... but each one is tempted when, by his own evil desire, he is dragged away and enticed. Then, after desire has conceived, it gives birth to sin; and sin, when it is full-grown, gives birth to death. **James 1:14-15**

Therefore, rid yourselves of all malice and all deceit, hypocrisy, envy, and slander of every kind....

... Christ suffered for you, leaving you an example, that you should follow in his steps.

"He committed no sin,
and no deceit was found in his mouth." **1 Peter 2:1, 21**

Therefore, my brothers, be all the more eager to make your calling and election sure. For if you do these things, you will never fall, and you will receive a rich welcome into the eternal kingdom of our Lord and Savior Jesus Christ.

So I will always remind you of these things, even though you know them and are firmly established in the truth you now have. **2 Peter 1:10-12**

If we claim to be without sin, we deceive ourselves and the truth is not in us. **1 John 1:8**

Dear friends, do not believe every spirit, but test the spirits to see whether they are from God, because many false prophets have gone out into the world. This is how you can recognize the Spirit of God: Every spirit that acknowledges that Jesus Christ has come in the flesh is from God, but every spirit that does not acknowledge Jesus is not from God. This is the spirit of the antichrist, which you have heard is coming and even now is already in the world. **1 John 4:1-3**

And the devil, who deceived them, was thrown into the lake of burning sulfur, where the beast and the false prophet had been thrown. They will be tormented day and night for ever and ever. **Revelation 20:10**

A PRAYER AGAINST DECEPTION

O Lord, how easy it is to be deceived! Help me to walk in your ways and obey your voice. Keep me from error, Lord. I cry out to you, knowing that I must trust you to guide and speak. Father, forgive me for the times in the past when I did not heed that still, small voice of warning. Help me to be more sensitive and attuned to your Spirit. In Jesus' wonderful name, Amen.

25

Standing against Verbal Attack

W HO AMONG US HAS NOT BEEN HARASSED by a boss, neighbor, or relative? Who hasn't felt betrayed by a friend? Or unfairly treated or falsely accused by a teacher, supervisor, or even a church leader? Some of us have even been the target of an unfounded lawsuit.

Some can identify with this Scripture: "Even my close friend, whom I trusted,/ he who shared my bread,/ has lifted up his heel against me" (Psalm 41:9). Certainly Jesus could. Just think, he knew beforehand that Judas, one of his inner circle of friends, would betray him. Jesus said in the garden of Gethsemane: "Rise, let us go! Here comes my betrayer!" (Matthew 26:46).

Yet even he who was betrayed gave us a noble example for responding to our enemies:

"You have heard that it was said, 'Love your neighbor and hate your enemy.' But I tell you: Love your enemies and pray for those who persecute you, that you may be sons of your Father in heaven...." **Matthew 5:43-45**

"And when you stand praying, if you hold anything against anyone, forgive him, so that your Father in heaven may forgive you your sins." **Mark 11:25**

Jesus took care to warn his followers about persecution: "'I tell you the truth,' Jesus replied, 'no one who has left home or brothers or sisters or mother or father or children or fields for me and the gospel will fail to receive a hundred times as much in this present age (homes, brothers, sisters, mothers, children and fields—and with them, persecutions) and in the age to come, eternal life'" (Mark 10:29-30).

The Apostle Paul learned this lesson well. He could write the church at Corinth: "That is why, for Christ's sake, I delight in weaknesses, in insults, in hardships, in persecutions, in difficulties. For when I am weak, then I am strong" (2 Corinthians 12:10). Let's examine some biblical examples of harassment or false accusation to strengthen our own spiritual battles against persecution.

TURNING THE TABLES

In the Book of Esther we read of Haman, who plotted to have the Jews within the Persian Empire annihilated. But Queen Esther called her people to fast and pray for their protection. This regal lady then risked her life by presenting herself to her husband without having been called. He was pleased with her and listened to her plea. As Esther unfolded Haman's wicked scheme, his plan backfired: "But when the plot came to the king's attention, he issued written orders that the evil scheme Haman had devised against the Jews should come back onto his own head, and that he and his sons should be hanged on the gallows" (Esther 9:25).

While busy rebuilding the broken walls around Jerusalem,

Nehemiah was continually harassed by Sanballat and his friends, who did everything to stop the work. But Nehemiah prayed for God's strength and refused to negotiate with his enemies. The result: "So the wall was completed... in fifty-two days. When all our enemies heard about this, all the surrounding nations were afraid and lost their self-confidence, because they realized that this work had been done with the help of our God" (Nehemiah 6:15-16).

Joseph's life reveals a litany of betrayal and false accusations by those close to him—from his own brothers, to his slave-master's wife, to his fellow prisoners. This innocent fellow must have felt completely deserted, but somehow he resisted giving in to bitterness. Eventually God rescued him and showered him with favor. Joseph became Prime Minister of Egypt, the land of his exile.

When his brothers who had betrayed him came to Egypt for food, Joseph showed no malice. He was able to say to them:

> And now, do not be distressed and do not be angry with yourselves for selling me here, because it was to save lives that God sent me ahead of you.... But God sent me ahead of you to preserve for you a remnant on earth and to save your lives by a great deliverance. So then it was not you who sent me here, but God. **Genesis 45:5-8**

Not only does God come to our rescue when we are harassed. Because we belong to him, his favor shines upon us. You may feel you have been misunderstood and never had your name or reputation cleared. But God is the one who keeps the records, not our fellow human beings.

We need to remember to turn to our heavenly Father for strength and wisdom in the midst of verbal attack. He will truly enable us to love our enemies and pray for them. Who knows? Perhaps the verbal attack is the very crack in the door through which Jesus can enter your accuser's heart. Seize the opportunity to do spiritual battle for the Lord.

SCRIPTURES

Contend, O LORD, with those who contend with me;
    fight against those who fight against me.
Take up shield and buckler;
    arise and come to my aid. **Psalm 35:1-2**

He rescued me from my powerful enemy,
    from my foes, who were too strong for me. **Psalm 18:17**

" ... no weapon forged against you will prevail,
    and you will refute every tongue that accuses you.
This is the heritage of the servants of the LORD,
    and this is their vindication from me," declares the LORD.
                                  Isaiah 54:17

On the contrary:
    "If your enemy is hungry, feed him;
        if he is thirsty, give him something to drink.
    In doing this, you will heap burning coals on his head."
                                  Romans 12:20

Yet do not regard him as an enemy, but warn him as a
brother. **2 Thessalonians 3:15**

for he guards the course of the just
    and protects the way of his faithful ones....
Wisdom will save you from the ways of wicked men,
    from men whose words are perverse.... **Proverbs 2:8, 12**

Do not accuse a man for no reason—
    when he has done you no harm. **Proverbs 3:30**

There are six things the LORD hates,
    seven that are detestable to him:
        Haughty eyes,
        a lying tongue,
        hands that shed innocent blood,
        a heart that devises wicked schemes,

feet that are quick to rush into evil,
a false witness who pours out lies
and a man who stirs up dissension among brothers.
Proverbs 6:16-19

The name of the LORD is a strong tower;
the righteous run to it and are safe.   **Proverbs 18:10**

Truthful lips endure forever,
but a lying tongue lasts only a moment....
The LORD detests lying lips,
but he delights in men who are truthful.   **Proverbs 12:19, 22**

When a man's ways are pleasing to the LORD
he makes even his enemies live at peace with him.
Proverbs 16:7

Do not testify against your neighbor without cause,
or use your lips to deceive.
Do not say, "I'll do to him as he has done to me;
I'll pay that man back for what he did."   **Proverbs 24:28-29**

Though they plot evil against you
and devise wicked schemes, they cannot succeed....
Psalm 21:11

Teach me your way, O LORD;
lead me in a straight path
because of my oppressors.
Do not turn me over to the desire of my foes,
for false witnesses rise up against me,
breathing out violence.   **Psalm 27:11-12**

Vindicate me, O God,
and plead my cause against an ungodly nation;
rescue me from deceitful and wicked men.   **Psalm 43:1**

My times are in your hands;
deliver me from my enemies
and from those who pursue me....

Let their lying lips be silenced,
    for with pride and contempt
    they speak arrogantly against the righteous.

How great is your goodness,
    which you have stored up for those who fear you,
which you bestow in the sight of men
    on those who take refuge in you.
In the shelter of your presence you hide them
    from the intrigues of men;
in your dwelling you keep them safe
    from accusing tongues.   **Psalm 31:15, 18-20**

You are my hiding place;
you will protect me from trouble
and surround me with songs of deliverance.   **Psalm 32:7**

Those who look to him are radiant;
    their faces are never covered with shame.   **Psalm 34:5**

Vindicate me in your righteousness, O LORD my God;
    do not let them gloat over me.
Do not let them think, "Aha, just what we wanted!"
    or say, "We have swallowed him up."   **Psalm 35:24-25**

… Deliver me from my enemies, O God;
    protect me from those who rise up against me.
Deliver me from evildoers
    and save me from bloodthirsty men.

See how they lie in wait for me!
    Fierce men conspire against me
    for no offense or sin of mine, O LORD.
I have done no wrong, yet they are ready to attack me.
    Arise to help me; look on my plight!   **Psalm 59:1-4**

For the LORD will vindicate his people
and have compassion on his servants.   **Psalm 135:14**

Because the LORD revealed their plot to me, I knew it, for at that time he showed me what they were doing.   Jeremiah 11:18

Whatever they plot against the LORD
　　he will bring to an end;
　　　　trouble will not come a second time.   Nahum 1:9

" ... do not plot evil against your neighbor, and do not love to swear falsely. I hate all this," declares the LORD.   Zechariah 8:17

Then the Pharisees went out and began to plot with the Herodians how they might kill Jesus.   Mark 3:6

Live such good lives among the pagans that, though they accuse you of doing wrong, they may see your good deeds and glorify God on the day he visits us.   1 Peter 2:12

SCRIPTURES ON RECEIVING GOD'S FAVOR

But Noah found favor in the eyes of the LORD.   Genesis 6:8

But while Joseph was there in the prison, the LORD was with him; he showed him kindness and granted him favor in the eyes of the prison warden.   Genesis 39:20b-21

But Moses sought the favor of the LORD his God. "O LORD," he said, "why should your anger burn against your people, whom you brought out of Egypt with great power and a mighty hand?"...

"If you are pleased with me, teach me your ways so I may know you and continue to find favor with you. Remember that this nation is your people."   Exodus 32:11; 33:13

"I will look on you with favor and make you fruitful and increase your numbers, and I will keep my covenant with you...."   Leviticus 26:9

For surely, O LORD, you bless the righteous;
  you surround them with your favor as with a shield. **Psalm 5:12**

For the LORD God is a sun and shield;
  the LORD bestows favor and honor;
no good thing does he withhold
  from those whose walk is blameless.   **Psalm 84:11**

For whoever finds me finds life
  and receives favor from the LORD. **Proverbs 8:35**

A good man obtains favor from the LORD,
  but the LORD condemns a crafty man.   **Proverbs 12:2**

This is what the LORD says:
  "In the time of my favor I will answer you,
    and in the day of salvation I will help you;
  I will keep you and will make you
    to be a covenant for the people,
  to restore the land
    and to reassign its desolate inheritances...."   **Isaiah 49:8**

"Arise, shine, for your light has come,
  and the glory of the LORD rises upon you.
See, darkness covers the earth
  and thick darkness is over the peoples,
but the LORD rises upon you
  and his glory appears over you....
"... Though in anger I struck you,
  in favor I will show you compassion."   **Isaiah 60:1-2, 10**

Now God had caused the official to show favor and sympathy
to Daniel....   **Daniel 1:9**

"The Lord has done this for me," she said. "In these days he
has shown his favor and taken away my disgrace among the
people." **Luke 1:25**

But the angel said to her, "Do not be afraid, Mary, you have found favor with God." **Luke 1:30**

"Glory to God in the highest,
   and on earth peace to men on whom his favor rests."

                                     Luke 2:14

And Jesus grew in wisdom and stature, and in favor with God and men. **Luke 2:52**

A PRAYER AGAINST HARASSMENT OR FALSE ACCUSATION

Father, thank you that no tongue that speaks against me shall do me permanent harm. My reputation, my life is in your hands. My hope is in you, Lord. You defend me like a shield. You are my stronghold and my deliverer. You bestow favor. You care for your children. Thank you, thank you, thank you for your loving favor. Amen!

26

Praying for Spiritual Leaders

WE CAN LEARN MORE ABOUT EFFECTIVE spiritual warfare by studying battles in the natural realm. For example, the general who devises superior strategy usually defeats his enemy. History is full of such examples. If a military general can somehow weaken the resolve of the leaders of the opposing forces, his side is much more likely to win the conflict.

We see these principles paralleled in the supernatural realm. Consider this observation by William Gurnall:

Two periods stand out in Christ's life: his entrance into public ministry at his baptism, and the culmination of it at his passion. At both he had a fierce encounter with the devil. This should give you an idea of how the master tempter works.... The more eminent your service for God, the greater the probability that Satan is at that very moment hatching some deadly scheme against you. If even the cadet corps need to be armed against Satan's bullets of temptation, how much more the commanders and officers, who stand in the front line of battle![1]

Scripture alerts all believers: "Be self-controlled and alert. Your enemy the devil prowls around like a roaring lion looking for someone to devour" (1 Peter 5:8). Christians need to be constantly vigilant against spiritual attack on themselves or their loved ones. But those in positions of leadership sorely need our prayer support as well. Dr. C. Peter Wagner warns, "If [the devil] has a choice, he will devour a leader before he will devour anyone else. And he will use every weapon in his arsenal to do it."[2]

The Apostle Paul requested personal intercession in his letters five times. He valued it; indeed, he counted on it. Paul writes:

> I urge you, brothers, by our Lord Jesus Christ and by the love of the Spirit, to join me in my struggle by praying to God for me. **Romans 15:30**

> On him [God] we have set our hope that he will continue to deliver us, as you help us by your prayers. Then many will give thanks on our behalf for the gracious favor granted us in answer to the prayers of many. **2 Corinthians 1:10-11**

> Pray also for me that whenever I open my mouth, words may be given me so that I will fearlessly make known the mystery of the gospel.... **Ephesians 6:19**

PASTORS NEED INTERCESSORS

Dr. Wagner's recent research leads him to conclude that Christian leaders and pastors need intercession even more than ordinary members of the Body of Christ. In his book, *Prayer Shield*, he cites several reasons:

1. *Pastors have more responsibility and accountability:* All Christians will come before the judgment seat of Christ, but pastors and other leaders have been forewarned that there is a divine double standard. One for "teachers" and one for all the rest. [See James 3:1.]

   ... When an office such as pastor or teacher (including seminary professor) has been granted by God and recognized by the Christian community, it is a grievous offense to break that trust.

2. *Pastors are more subject to temptation:* The higher up you go on the ladder of Christian leadership, the higher you go on Satan's hit list.... Satan uses the world. He tempts pastors with greed, power and pride....

   Satan uses the flesh [i.e. illicit sex, pornography, gluttony, alcohol, substance abuse].

   Satan also uses "the devil." This means demonization, spells, curses, and incantations.

   ... Satan is more specific, persistent and intentional when it comes to pastors and other leaders.

3. *Pastors are targets of spiritual warfare:* Over the last several years Satanists, witches, New Agers, occult practitioners, shamans, spiritists and other servants of darkness have entered into an evil covenant to pray to Satan for the breakdown of marriages of pastors and Christian leaders....

4. *Pastors have more influence on others:* If a pastor falls, more people are hurt and set back in their spiritual lives than if others fall. The ripple effect is incredibly devastating. Strong Christians are crushed by the hypocrisy and betrayal they feel. Weak Christians take the pastor's behavior as a license for them to do likewise....

5. *Pastors have more visibility:* Because pastors are up front, they are constantly subject to gossip and criticism.... Just knowing this places a difficult burden on pastors and they need supernatural help to handle that situation well. Intercession opens the way for them to receive this help.[3]

SAFEGUARDS FOR INTERCESSORS

Many pastors are wary of allowing intercessory prayer groups to function in the church because of potential problems. Of course the enemy will try to incite trouble in order to discredit the value of intercession. But the wise pastor will establish prayer as an important priority by his own example, and set up safeguards to prevent excessive zeal.

Once in a while an individual will join an intercessors' group who prays in a selfish or controlling way, or who prays with impure motives. Cindy Jacobs, in her book *Possessing the Gates of the Enemy*, describes "flaky intercessors" as:

> ... Men and women who for a variety of reasons, drift outside biblical guidelines in their zeal for prayer. They bring reproach on their ministries and confusion and division in the church.
>
> ... Many aspiring intercessors pray out of bitterness and woundedness. What I find remarkable is that they are unaware of these heart conditions. They are drawn to intercession because of its great power and, subconsciously, because they see it as a means of getting their way.... A good prayer for intercessors, therefore, is "Lord, show me my heart so that I can remain pure before you always."[4]

GUIDELINES FOR DAILY PRAYER

Many prayer warriors find it helpful to pray for the needs of spiritual leaders by targeting specific areas each day of the week. Elizabeth Alves, President of Intercessors International, suggests in her *Prayer Manual* daily categories like praying for spiritual leaders, missionaries, and ministers. Generally her outline follows this pattern:

Sunday   Favor with God: spiritual revelation, anointing, holiness (see Psalm 90:17).

Monday	Favor with man: congregation, staff, those who don't know Christ (see Acts 2:47).
Tuesday	Increased vision: wisdom, enlightenment, motives, guidance (see Habakkuk 2:2).
Wednesday	Spirit, soul, body: that we would be complete in every way (see 1 Thessalonians 5:23).
Thursday	Protection: against temptation, deception, plans of the enemy (see Psalm 91).
Friday	Finances: priorities, blessings (see Proverbs 8:17-18, 21; Luke 6:38).
Saturday	Family: unity, spiritual life, spouse, children (see Acts 16:32; Joshua 24:15; Matthew 6:31-34; Psalm 25:12-15).[5]

PRAYING FOR MISSIONARIES

1. Pray that God will send angels to guard over them in their travels (see Psalm 91), and that he will make a hedge to protect their family, property, and possessions.
2. That the Lord will send angels before them to do battle on their behalf (see Psalm 78:49).
3. That all attacks and traps of the enemy be foiled, and the missionaries kept from the nets of the enemy while they walk by safely (see Psalm 141:9-10).
4. That God be their hiding place and preserve them from trouble, surrounding them with songs of deliverance (see Psalm 32:7).
5. For sensitivity to the Holy Spirit, and a spirit of wisdom and revelation (see Ephesians 1:17).
6. That the Word of God go forth as a double-edged sword, judging the thoughts and attitudes of the hearts of the hearers (see Hebrews 4:12).
7. That the missionaries be anointed "to preach good news to the poor/... to bind up the brokenhearted, / to proclaim freedom for the captives / and release from darkness for the prisoners" (Isaiah 61:1).

8. That the Word fall on hearts open to hear and obey the Lord (see Luke 8:15), and that the enemy not steal the Word after it is sown (see Luke 8:12).

VULNERABLE TARGETS

In his appeal for more intercession and spiritual warfare on behalf of spiritual leaders, Dr. Wagner says:

The enemy knows that pastors... are vulnerable, and he attacks at their weakest point. This is not to say that those who have fallen are not themselves guilty and do not have character flaws which need to be repaired through humility, repentance, reconciliation, restoration and holiness. But I do hope and pray that we will learn how to use our spiritual weapons more effectively in putting a stop to these blatant and all too successful attacks of the devil.[6]

The media love to report alleged scandals and failures in the lives of high-profile ministers and televangelists. In addition, probably every person who reads this book knows personally one or more spiritual leaders who have fallen into the enemy's trap of moral failure. Especially when a leader takes a tumble, the diligent spiritual warrior should continue to pray for that individual and for all the people affected by the tragedy.

On the heels of such a fiasco, the devil works on those who feel hurt, betrayed, or disappointed, tempting them to give in to cynicism and bitterness. But the true intercessor will stand in the gap against Satan's attempts to destroy the faith of the wounded ones. He or she will also cry out to God for the fallen leader's restoration. No matter how devastating a situation seems to be, the persistent prayer warrior affirms that God can take what the devil meant for evil and turn it to good (see Genesis 50:20).

Several other sections of this book—especially chapter 22,

Battling against Deception—provide guidelines and Scriptures to pray for leaders. Use the sword of the Spirit and the weapons of the blood of Jesus and praise to push back Satan's assaults against spiritual leaders.

SAMUEL'S INTERCESSION

The prophet Samuel is an example of an intercessor who prayed for a nation and for its leader. On one occasion the Israelites heard that the Philistines had assembled and were going to attack them. They begged Samuel: "Do not stop crying out to the LORD our God for us, that he may rescue us from the hand of the Philistines" (1 Samuel 7:8).

Later Israel demanded—against God's plan—that Samuel appoint a king to rule over them. The prophet knew their sin of rebellion meant trouble. But he wisely informed them: "As for me, far be it from me that I should sin against the LORD by failing to pray for you..." (1 Samuel 12:23).

On another occasion, Samuel agonized over Saul's disobedience: "Then Samuel left for Ramah, but Saul went up to his home in Gibeah of Saul. Until the day Samuel died, he did not go to see Saul again, though Samuel mourned for him. And the LORD was grieved that he had made Saul king over Israel" (1 Samuel 15:34-35).

SCRIPTURES

Then the word of the LORD came to Samuel: "I am grieved that I have made Saul king, because he has turned away from me and has not carried out my instructions." Samuel was troubled, and he cried out to the LORD all that night. 1 Samuel 15:10-11

Pray in the Spirit on all occasions with all kinds of prayers and requests. With this in mind, be alert and always keep on praying for all the saints. Ephesians 6:18

I have not stopped giving thanks for you, remembering you in my prayers. Ephesians 1:16

I thank my God every time I remember you. In all my prayers for all of you, I always pray with joy because of your partnership in the gospel from the first day until now, being confident of this, that he who began a good work in you will carry it on to completion until the day of Christ Jesus. Philippians 1:3-6

We always thank God for all of you, mentioning you in our prayers. 1 Thessalonians 1:2

Now I want you to know, brothers, that what has happened to me has really served to advance the gospel. As a result, it has become clear throughout the whole palace guard and to everyone else that I am in chains for Christ....
... for I know that through your prayers and the help given by the Spirit of Jesus Christ, what has happened to me will turn out for my deliverance. Philippians 1:12-13, 19

I urge, then, first of all, that requests, prayers, intercession and thanksgiving be made for everyone—for kings and all those in authority, that we may live peaceful and quiet lives in all godliness and holiness. This is good, and pleases God our Savior.... 1 Timothy 2:1-3

I thank God, whom I serve, as my forefathers did, with a clear conscience, as night and day I constantly remember you in my prayers. 2 Timothy 1:3

I always thank my God as I remember you in my prayers.... I pray that you may be active in sharing your faith, so that you will have a full understanding of every good thing we have in Christ. Philemon 4, 6

During the days of Jesus' life on earth, he offered up prayers and petitions with loud cries and tears to the one who could save him from death, and he was heard because of his reverent submission. **Hebrews 5:7**

Husbands,... be considerate as you live with your wives, and treat them with respect as the weaker partner and as heirs with you of the gracious gift of life, so that nothing will hinder your prayers. **1 Peter 3:7**

I will be careful to lead a blameless life—
    when will you come to me?
I will walk in my house
    with blameless heart. **Psalm 101:2**

May my heart be blameless toward your decrees,
    that I may not be put to shame. **Psalm 119:80**

He whose walk is blameless is kept safe,
    but he whose ways are perverse will suddenly fall.
                    Proverbs 28:18

This service that you perform is not only supplying the needs of God's people but is also overflowing in many expressions of thanks to God.... And in their prayers for you their hearts will go out to you, because of the surpassing grace God has given you. **2 Corinthians 9:12, 14**

May he strengthen your hearts so that you will be blameless and holy in the presence of our God and Father when our Lord Jesus comes with all his holy ones. **1 Thessalonians 3:13**

An elder must be blameless, the husband of but one wife, a man whose children believe and are not open to the charge of being wild and disobedient. **Titus 1:6**

Since an overseer is entrusted with God's work, he must be blameless—not overbearing, not quick-tempered, not given to drunkenness, not violent, not pursuing dishonest gain.
                    Titus 1:7

So then, dear friends, since you are looking forward to this, make every effort to be found spotless, blameless and at peace with him. **2 Peter 3:14**

May God himself, the God of peace, sanctify you through and through. May your whole spirit, soul and body be kept blameless at the coming of our Lord Jesus Christ. **1 Thessalonians 5:23**

27

Mobilizing
Prayer Groups

I N ANCIENT TIMES, soldiers served as watchmen on the wall. Keeping guard over a city was absolutely essential to the safety of the inhabitants. These soldiers were the "early warning system" for the armies of that era.

Today's intercessors serve as the modern counterpart to watchmen. In the spiritual realm, they serve as the radar system for the Body of Christ. Within the ranks of church congregations, intercessors are mobilizing into prayer groups in increasing numbers. They meet to pray for their leaders and for the congregation, and for whatever is on God's heart when they come together.

A watchman must be mentally alert, observant, vigilant. He guards and protects, and keeps alert to the enemy's schemes to ward them off or to warn others. He remains constantly on the lookout during his "watch" or assigned shift.

In biblical times watchmen were positioned not only on the city wall, but also in a watchtower—located either in a field or a vineyard. Jamie Buckingham parallels these towers with our own situation:

> The watchtower was a familiar sight in Jesus' day. Built of the stones taken from a field, it usually sat in the middle of a field or a vineyard.
>
> ... At night the watchmen would take turns during various "watches" of the night to guard the field—protecting it from foxes, bears, and poachers.
>
> In Old Testament days these towers were used by military watchmen. The soldiers would be looking out for the Philistines, fierce bands of renegades who would wait until the crops were ripe, then swoop down to harvest what another man had cultivated.
>
> ... You may not think your little field is very important. But God has set you in your field as a watchman. Each one of us has a sphere of influence. Most of us don't realize it, but our influence is much larger than we can ever imagine —and will continue on for generations to come, be it good or evil. It's a wonderful responsibility—frightening at times —but wonderful. Always remember, though, you're never in your watchtower alone. Jesus is ever with you, and his Spirit will whisper just the things you need to say and do.[1]

Take your places as watchmen in the tower where God has placed you, confident that as you focus your trust upon him, he will direct your intercession to hit the target.

GUIDELINES FOR PRAYER GROUP LEADERS

How do you identify a prayer leader? Cindy Jacobs, who has mobilized prayer watches in numerous countries, heads up Generals of Intercession. This highly seasoned prayer warrior suggests looking for the following attributes in a potential prayer leader:

- The ability to lead prayer (preferably with the gift of intercession).

- A good working relationship with other leaders.
- A teachable spirit and a servant's heart.
- An ability to lead without controlling.
- No evidence of a critical spirit.
- A proven gift of intercession which has been tested by accuracy and effectiveness (do they have "right on" prayers and do they see many answers?).[2]

Cindy further suggests guidelines for intercessory prayer group leaders:

1. Ask the Lord for his focus.
2. Seek the Lord's will as to how he wants the focus implemented. This might include:
   - Petition prayers (petitioning God for the needs).
   - Proclamation prayers (proclaiming the attributes of the Lord concerning the needs).
   - Intercessory praise.
   - Prophetic intercession.
   - Scripture praying.
3. Spend time before the Lord personally and make sure you are walking in forgiveness toward those in your prayer group and church.
4. Talk to your pastor or ministry leader and ask for any prayer requests or direction.[3]

During corporate prayer time, Cindy urges the leader of the group to make sure each prayer request is "prayed through" until there is a release from the Lord. Then keep the momentum moving, keeping these things in mind:

1. Discourage one person from being a "prayer hog" and taking all the prayer time.
2. Instruct intercessors to listen for God's direction with one ear, and to the prayers others are praying with the other. Being sensitive to both will keep individuals from diverting the general flow of the Spirit's direction.

266 / The Spiritual Warrior's Prayer Guide

3. Notice whether some in the group have a physical hearing loss. If so, they need to sit near the prayer leader.
4. Keep the prayer focused.... Ask members to stay on one track until the leader switches to another need.
5. Bring correction if needed.... Meet the individual after the meeting. Pray first and determine whether the person will hear correction directly from the Lord without your having to speak to them.
6. Assess the spiritual maturity of your group.[4]

ESTABLISHING A PRAYER GROUP[5]

Each church congregation must prayerfully determine what type of intercession program will work best for them. Once a prayer group is established, confidentiality must be stressed within the ranks of those praying together. How often they pray, where they pray, and the main focus of prayer should be decided at the outset. Will the main thrust be to pray for the church and its members' needs? Or will it include praying for the community or nation? For missionaries? For those who don't yet know Christ? For the sick, homeless, unemployed?

How will prayer requests be received? Will the last names of those being prayed for be kept anonymous? Will records of answered prayer be kept? Will a crisis line be set up so that members can be called at any time for emergency needs?

One of the key spiritual leaders (pastor or board member) should be involved in the establishment of the ministry. The group also needs to maintain some type of accountability to that church leader.

CALL THE CHURCH TO PRAYER

Once an intercessory prayer group is functioning within a church, the whole congregation usually becomes more aware of the importance of prayer. When the leadership suggests specific guidelines for prayer each month, effectiveness is strengthened when everyone can focus on the same prayer needs. Here's an example from a church bulletin:

For the Church:
1. Continue to press into a position to hear God's voice (Psalm 85:8). Pray for breakthroughs in the following areas:
    a) Strengthening of marriages
    b) Release of our singles into fullness of opportunity in the Kingdom
    c) Healing and a hedge of physical protection
2. Pray for our missionaries.

For the State:
Pray for our state governmental leaders to make godly decisions in the following areas (Psalm 146:9):
    a) Sodomy law
    b) Abortion issues
    c) Textbook selection

International Concerns:
Pray for the nation of Israel (Zechariah 2:8). Pray that the Christians there will have greater penetration into the life of the nation.

SCRIPTURES

I have posted watchmen on your walls, O Jerusalem;
    they will never be silent day or night.
You who call on the LORD,
    give yourselves no rest,
and give him no rest till he establishes Jerusalem
    and makes her the praise of the earth.   **Isaiah 62:6-7**

"But if the watchman sees the sword coming and does not blow the trumpet to warn the people and the sword comes and takes the life of one of them, that man will be taken away because of his sin, but I will hold the watchman accountable for his blood.

Son of man, I have made you a watchman for the house of Israel; so hear the word I speak and give them warning from me.   **Ezekiel 33:6-7**

Joshua said to the Israelites, "Come here and listen to the words of the LORD your God."   **Joshua 3:9**

So Joshua... chose thirty thousand of his best fighting men and sent them out at night with these orders: "Listen carefully. You are to set an ambush behind the city. Don't go very far from it. All of you be on the alert."   **Joshua 8:3, 4**

May your eyes be open to your servant's plea and to the plea of your people Israel, and may you listen to them whenever they cry out to you....   **1 Kings 8:52**

Give ear, O LORD, and hear; open your eyes, O LORD, and see; listen to the words Sennacherib has sent to insult the living God.   **2 Kings 19:16**

Listen to my cry for help,
     my King and my God,
        for to you I pray.   **Psalm 5:2**

You hear, O LORD, the desire of the afflicted;
     you encourage them, and you listen to their cry.   **Psalm 10:17**

A voice came from the cloud, saying, "This is my Son, whom I have chosen; listen to him."   **Luke 9:35**

I will instruct you and teach you in the way you should go;
     I will counsel you and watch over you.   **Psalm 32:8**

Set a guard over my mouth, O LORD;
     keep watch over the door of my lips.   **Psalm 141:3**

An attacker advances against you, [Nineveh].
Guard the fortress,
watch the road,
brace yourselves,
marshal all your strength! Nahum 2:1

Look at the nations and watch—
and be utterly amazed.
For I am going to do something in your days
that you would not believe,
even if you were told. Habakkuk 1:5

I will stand at my watch
and station myself on the ramparts;
I will look to see what he will say to me,
and what answer I am to give to this complaint. Habakkuk 2:1

But I will defend my house
against marauding forces.
Never again will an oppressor overrun my people,
for now I am keeping watch. Zechariah 9:8

"Watch out for false prophets. They come to you in sheep's clothing, but inwardly they are ferocious wolves." Matthew 7:15

Jesus answered: "Watch out that no one deceives you."
Matthew 24:4

"Therefore keep watch, because you do not know on what day your Lord will come. But understand this: If the owner of the house had known at what time of night the thief was coming, he would have kept watch and would not have let his house be broken into." Matthew 24:42-43

Then he said to them, "My soul is overwhelmed with sorrow to the point of death. Stay here and keep watch with me."
Matthew 26:38

"Watch and pray so that you will not fall into temptation. The spirit is willing, but the body is weak." **Matthew 26:41**

What I say to you, I say to everyone: "Watch!"   **Mark 13:37**

Then he returned to his disciples and found them sleeping. "Simon," he said to Peter, "are you asleep? Could you not keep watch for one hour? Watch and pray so that you will not fall into temptation. The spirit is willing, but the body is weak."   **Mark 14:37-38**

And there were shepherds living out in the fields nearby, keeping watch over their flocks at night.   **Luke 2:8**

Then he said to them, "Watch out! Be on your guard against all kinds of greed; a man's life does not consist in the abundance of his possessions."   **Luke 12:15**

"It will be good for those servants whose master finds them ready, even if he comes in the second or third watch of the night."   **Luke 12:38**

"So watch yourselves.
    "If your brother sins, rebuke him, and if he repents, forgive him...."   **Luke 17:3**

"Be always on the watch, and pray that you may be able to escape all that is about to happen, and that you may be able to stand before the Son of Man."   **Luke 21:36**

I urge you, brothers, to watch out for those who cause divisions and put obstacles in your way that are contrary to the teaching you have learned. Keep away from them.   **Romans 16:17**

Brothers, if someone is caught in a sin, you who are spiritual should restore him gently. But watch yourself, or you also may be tempted.   **Galatians 6:1**

So then, let us not be like others, who are asleep, but let us be alert and self-controlled.   **1 Thessalonians 5:6**

Watch your life and doctrine closely. Persevere in them, because if you do, you will save both yourself and your hearers.   **1 Timothy 4:16**

Obey your leaders and submit to their authority. They keep watch over you as men who must give an account. Obey them so that their work will be a joy, not a burden, for that would be of no advantage to you.   **Hebrews 13:17**

Watch out that you do not lose what you have worked for, but that you may be rewarded fully.   **2 John 1:8**

28

Praying for Your Neighborhood, City, and Nation

FROM THE TIME HE CALLED Abraham and promised to make a nation of him, God intended his people to be a means of blessing other nations of the earth. Note these verses:

Abraham will surely become a great and powerful nation, and all nations on earth will be blessed through him.

Genesis 18:18

"... seek the peace and prosperity of the city to which I have carried you into exile. Pray to the LORD for it, because if it prospers, you too will prosper.... For I know the plans I have for you," declares the LORD, "plans to prosper you and not to harm you, plans to give you hope and a future."

Jeremiah 29:7, 11

God exhorts all of us to pray for the peace and prosperity of the city and region where we live. He also directs individual intercessors to pray for cities and nations where our feet have never walked. But in prayer we can "possess the land," so that God's purposes can be fulfilled and the gospel proclaimed in those areas.

As we pray we must recognize that Satan blinds people to the truth of the gospel. Spiritual warfare is required to tear down strongholds of deception and unbelief to enable the people to hear the Word. The Apostle Paul wrote: "And even if our gospel is veiled, it is veiled to those who are perishing. The god of this age has blinded the minds of unbelievers, so that they cannot see the light of the gospel of the glory of Christ..." (2 Corinthians 4:3-4).

Since Satan can only be in one place at a time, how can he possibly blind the minds of the approximately three billion people in this world who have yet to receive the gospel of Jesus? By delegating this responsibility to evil spirits, explains Dr. C. Peter Wagner, a missions professor at Fuller Theological Seminary. He writes:

> The hypothesis I am suggesting is that Satan delegates high ranking members of the hierarchy of evil spirits to control nations, regions, cities, tribes, people groups, neighborhoods and other significant social networks of human beings throughout the world. Their major assignment is to prevent God from being glorified in their territory, which they do through directing the activity of lower ranking demons.[1]

Once we understand how demonic forces are hindering God's work, believers have the authority to break the control of those spirits through prayer and fasting. First, we declare we have the blood of Jesus over us before we engage in warfare. Then we pull down strongholds—an offensive warfare action—assailing the powers of darkness that keep souls in continued bondage.

Again, we clarify our strategy while in prayer. God may show us that certain evil spirits or principalities are causing an area to be ruled by greed, intellectualism, witchcraft, pride, traditions, poverty, or whatever. We can then assault these specific strongholds through prayer.

SPIRITUAL MAPPING

Scripture tells us that God himself set the boundaries to the nations: "When the Most High gave the nations their inheritance,/when he divided all mankind,/he set up boundaries for the peoples/ according to the number of the sons of Israel" (Deuteronomy 32:8).

Biblical scholars such as F.F. Bruce suggest that discoveries from the Dead Sea scrolls indicate that the correct translation of this passage should be: "according to the number of the angels of God." Bruce comments: "This reading implies that the administration of the various nations has been parceled out among a corresponding number of angelic powers.... In a number of places some at least of these angelic governors are portrayed as hostile principalities and powers—the 'world rulers of this darkness' of Ephesians 6:12."[2]

Daniel mentions "the prince of Persia" and "the prince of Greece"—spirits that dominated specific geographic areas. These spirit beings hindered God's angels while they were en route to give Daniel a message from God in answer to his prayer.

God once instructed the prophet Ezekiel: "... take a clay tablet, put it in front of you and draw the city of Jerusalem on it. Then lay siege to it:... Then take an iron pan and place it as an iron wall between you and the city and turn your face toward it. It will be under siege, and you shall besiege it. This will be a sign to the house of Israel" (Ezekiel 4:1-3).

A clay tablet was the equivalent of a piece of modern writing paper. Experienced intercessors interpret this passage to mean Ezekiel was to engage in a spiritual warfare tactic by praying over the city—not necessarily going to war against it.

Intercessors who believe in "spiritual mapping" often do historical research concerning the area of interest, looking for clues that will reveal the inroads Satan used to infiltrate that territory. They also study its Christian history in an attempt to build upon what the forefathers of faith began— especially during times of revival. They may also pray over maps of the area or walk the streets in prayer groups, after appropriate orientation and preparation.

RESEARCHING A CITY

Some evangelists send advance prayer teams into a city to pray and discern what strongholds are preventing its inhabitants from receiving the gospel message. Other evangelists closet themselves in a hotel room for days, doing spiritual warfare before opening crusades.

John Dawson, in *Taking Our Cities for God*, talks about researching the particular city where you live. The same principles he shares also apply to other cities or nations. Note the relevant questions:

Do you know your city? You should have the census in one hand and the Bible in the other. What percentage of people actually attend church? How many people are in poverty? Why are they in poverty? Where do they live? Are there subcultures, ethnic groups, changes in the economy, an aging problem? What's really going on? You need to know if you are going to help free your city from evil spiritual dominance.

First, get out a map of the city. Study it carefully. See if you can identify concentrations of the elderly, the homeless, students, children and so on. What subcultures are more receptive than others to the gospel? Why? What are the felt needs of the people of the city?... Parts of the city may vary greatly in culture, crime levels and wealth....

What you research depends on your goals. A pastor

planting a church or an evangelist planning an outreach will need very specific information and statistics. However, all of us are called to the ministry of interecession...."[3]

PRAYER STRATEGY FOR TARGETED CITIES

Barbara James suggests this prayer strategy for intercessors in your city:

John 3:30	Exaltation of Christ
John 4:35	Visions of Harvest
John 4:34	Commitment to God's Will/Work

For the lost in targeted cities:

| John 4:39-42 | Truth that Prevails[4] |

HOW TO PRAY FOR YOUR CITY

The following chart is a combination of ideas by Dr. C. Peter Wagner and John Dawson, published by Fuller Evangelistic Association in an effort to encourage corporate prayer for cities:

How to Pray for Your City

1. Determine the geographical boundaries of your city or the area about which you are especially concerned.
2. Secure the participation of pastors and other Christian leaders in the area and begin to pray together on a regular basis.
3. Assure the spiritual preparation of participating leaders and other Christians through repentance, humility, and holiness.
4. Project a clear image that this effort involves the whole Body of Christ—not just one local church, a single denomination, or an exclusive group.
5. Research the secular history of your city. Why is this city here and what moral and spiritual trends were involved in its founding?

6. Humbly identify the sins of your city which have become invisible barriers to the gospel, and call on God for mercy.

7. Look at your city's Christian people here, particularly during times of revival. Find out what God has revealed to our forefathers of faith.

8. Study your city's demographics. Where do people live? How many are in poverty and why? What are the trends? Get the facts.

9. Identify the present-day spiritual leaders and those with prophetic insight in your area. What are they saying about your city's problems, its needs, its future?

10. Work with intercessors especially gifted and called to strategic-level spiritual warfare, seeking God's timing and plan of attack on Satan's strongholds.

11. Once you know what you are up against, begin spiritiual warfare with worship. Exercise the authority of Jesus. Overcome evil with good; conquer pride with humility, lust with purity, fear with faith.

12. Travail in prayer until God's purposes are birthed and the gospel message breaks through, bringing spiritual revival to your city. God waits for a people who will see him as he is and follow him to victory.[5]

EXAMPLE OF ONE INTERCESSOR

One righteous man stood before God and interceded for the wicked city of Sodom. Abraham asked God if he would spare Sodom if he found fifty righteous people there. Yes. If only forty-five? Yes. If only forty? Thirty? Twenty? Finally, if there were only ten? God was willing. But the wicked city was destroyed. Obviously for lack of righteousness. Here's a capsule version of that account:

> Then the LORD said, "The outcry against Sodom and Gomorrah is so great and their sin so grievous....
> Then Abraham approached him and said, "Will you sweep away the righteous with the wicked? What if there

are fifty righteous people in the city? Will you really sweep it away and not spare the place for the sake of the fifty righteous people in it? Far be it from you to do such a thing—to kill the righteous with the wicked....

The LORD said, "If I find fifty righteous people in the city of Sodom, I will spare the whole place for their sake." ...

Then he [Abraham] said, "May the Lord not be angry, but let me speak just once more. What if only ten can be found there?"

He answered, "For the sake of ten, I will not destroy it."

Genesis 18:20, 23-26, 32

SCRIPTURES

"Turn to me and be saved,
    all you ends of the earth;
    for I am God, and there is no other.
By myself I have sworn,
    my mouth has uttered in all integrity
    a word that will not be revoked:
Before me every knee will bow;
    by me every tongue will swear.
They will say of me, 'In the LORD alone
    are righteousness and strength.'"
All who have raged against him
    will come to him and be put to shame.   **Isaiah 45:22-24**

"I have seen these people," the LORD said to Moses, "and they are a stiff-necked people. Now leave me alone so that my anger may burn against them and that I may destroy them. Then I will make you into a great nation."

But Moses sought the favor of the LORD his God. "O LORD," he said, "why should your anger burn against your people, whom you brought out of Egypt with great power and a mighty hand?... Turn from your fierce anger; relent and do not bring disaster on your people. Remember your servants Abraham, Isaac and Israel, to whom you swore by your own self: 'I will make your descendants as numerous as the stars in the sky and I will give your descendants all this land I promised them, and it will be their inheritance forever.'" Then the LORD relented and did not bring on his people the disaster he had threatened. **Exodus 32:9-14**

... if my people, who are called by my name, will humble themselves and pray and seek my face and turn from their wicked ways, then will I hear from heaven and will forgive their sin and will heal their land. **2 Chronicles 7:14**

Why do the nations conspire
   and the peoples plot in vain?
The kings of the earth take their stand
   and the rulers gather together
against the LORD
   and against his Anointed One.
"Let us break their chains," they say,
   "and throw off their fetters."

The One enthroned in heaven laughs;
   the Lord scoffs at them.
Then he rebukes them in his anger
   and terrifies them in his wrath, saying,
"I have installed my King
   on Zion, my holy hill."

I will proclaim the decree of the LORD:

He said to me, "You are my Son;
   today I have become your Father.
Ask of me,
   and I will make the nations your inheritance,
   the ends of the earth your possession." **Psalm 2:1-8**

He will judge the world in righteousness;
   he will govern the peoples with justice. **Psalm 9:8**

The LORD foils the plans of the nations;
   he thwarts the purposes of the peoples. **Psalm 33:10**

I will praise you, O LORD, among the nations;
　　I will sing of you among the peoples.
For great is your love, reaching to the heavens;
　　your faithfulness reaches to the skies.

Be exai ed, O God, above the heavens;
　　let your glory be over all the earth. **Psalm 57:9-11**

May God be gracious to us...
that your ways may be known on earth,
　　your salvation among all nations.

May the peoples praise you, O God;
　　may all the peoples praise you.
May the nations be glad and sing for joy,
　　for you rule the peoples justly
　　and guide the nations of the earth. **Psalm 67:1-4**

Your ways, O God, are holy.
　　What god is so great as our God?
You are the God who performs miracles;
　　you display your power among the peoples. **Psalm 77:13-14**

Oh, the raging of many nations—
　　they rage like the raging sea!
Oh, the uproar of the peoples—
　　they roar like the roaring of great waters!
Although the peoples roar like the roar of surging waters,
　　when [God] rebukes them they flee far away,
driven before the wind like chaff on the hills,
　　like tumbleweed before a gale. **Isaiah 17:12-13**

Woe to those who go down to Egypt for help,
　　who rely on horses,
who trust in the multitude of their chariots
　　and in the great strength of their horsemen,
but do not look to the Holy One of Israel,
　　or seek help from the LORD....
... the Egyptians are men and not God;

their horses are flesh and not spirit....
At the thunder of your voice, the peoples flee;
  when you rise up, the nations scatter.   Isaiah 31:1-3; 33:3

I have posted watchmen on your walls, O Jerusalem;
  they will never be silent day or night.
You who call on the LORD,
  give yourselves no rest,
and give him no rest till he establishes Jerusalem
  and makes her the praise of the earth.   Isaiah 62:6-7

"See, today I appoint you over nations and kingdoms to up-root and tear down, to destroy and overthrow, to build and to plant."   Jeremiah 1:10

Many nations will come and say,

"Come, let us go up to the mountain of the LORD,
  to the house of the God of Jacob.
He will teach us his ways,
  so that we may walk in his paths."
The law will go out from Zion,
  the word of the LORD from Jerusalem.
He will judge between many peoples
  and will settle disputes for strong nations far and wide.
They will beat their swords into plowshares
  and their spears into pruning hooks.
Nation will not take up sword against nation,
  nor will they train for war anymore.   Micah 4:2-3

"My name will be great among the nations, from the rising to the setting of the sun. In every place... my name will be great among the nations," says the LORD Almighty.   Malachi 1:11

"Ever since the time of your forefathers you have turned away from my decrees and have not kept them. Return to me, and I will return to you," says the LORD Almighty....   Malachi 3:7

Therefore God exalted [Christ] to the highest place
  and gave him the name that is above every name,

that at the name of Jesus every knee should bow,
    in heaven and on earth and under the earth,
and every tongue confess that Jesus Christ is Lord,
    to the glory of God the Father.   **Philippians 2:9-11**

Look, he is coming with the clouds,
    and every eye will see him,
even those who pierced him;
    and all the peoples of the earth will mourn because of him.
      So shall it be! Amen.   **Revelation 1:7**

Who will not fear you, O Lord,
    and bring glory to your name?
For you alone are holy.
All nations will come
    and worship before you,
for your righteous acts have been revealed.   **Revelation 15:4**

How awesome is the LORD Most High,
    the great King over all the earth!   **Psalm 47:2**

God reigns over the nations;
    God is seated on his holy throne.   **Psalm 47:8**

Ask of me,
    and I will make the nations your inheritance,
    the ends of the earth your possession.   **Psalm 2:8**

Therefore, you kings, be wise;
be warned, you rulers of the earth.   **Psalm 2:10**

When the righteous triumph, there is great elation;
but when the wicked rise to power, men go into hiding.
                                        Proverbs 28:12

Where there is no revelation, the people cast off restraint;
    but blessed is he who keeps the law.   **Proverbs 29:18**

We were with child, we writhed in pain,
    but we gave birth to wind.

We have not brought salvation to the earth;
   we have not given birth to people of the world.   **Isaiah 26:18**

LORD, I have heard of your fame;
   I stand in awe of your deeds, O LORD.
Renew them in our day,
   in our time make them known;
   in wrath remember mercy.   **Habakkuk 3:2**

Blow the trumpet in Zion,
   declare a holy fast,
   call a sacred assembly.
Gather the people,
   consecrate the assembly;
bring together the elders,
   gather the children,
   those nursing at the breast.
Let the bridegroom leave his room
   and the bride her chamber.
Let the priests, who minister before the LORD,
   weep between the temple porch and the altar.
Let them say, "Spare your people, O LORD.
   Do not make your inheritance an object of scorn,
   a byword among the nations.
Why should they say among the peoples,
   'Where is their God?'"

Then the LORD will be jealous for his land
   and take pity on his people.   **Joel 2:15-18**

They told him, "This is what Hezekiah says: This day is a day
of distress and rebuke and disgrace, as when children come to
the point of birth and there is no strength to deliver them. It
may be that the LORD your God will hear all the words of the
field commander, whom his master, the king of Assyria, has
sent to ridicule the living God, and that he will rebuke him for
the words the LORD your God has heard. Therefore pray for
the remnant that still survives."   **2 Kings 19:3-4**

Epilogue

Spiritual warfare is certainly valuable and effective at a personal level. It works for yourself, your children, your household. But God's plan is much bigger. It's worldwide!

More than a dozen years ago, I started out praying for my own children after Satan had lured them into his camp. My husband and I knew very little about spiritual warfare at that time. But we knew it was the devil's kingdom we were up against, and we knew the Word of God was our weapon. We quoted it as we battled. We claimed God's promises for our household and declared our children's sojourn in the enemy's camp was merely temporary.

The battle proved to be neither easy nor short. We travailed, wept, shouted, fasted, and held tightly onto the Word even when victory appeared to be hopeless. But finally we witnessed a breakthrough with the youngest. A godly young man for whom I had prayed for eight years challenged her to make a decision about her eternal destiny. She wept her way back to the Lord Jesus. Within eight months, her brother and sister had also recommitted their lives to the Lord. Today they all continue to serve him.

Little did I know how God would use what he was teaching me in the prayer closet. It would eventually lead to an expanded vision of praying for other young people, spiritual leaders, cities, even nations.

In my own neighborhood and town, I have walked the streets praying, often with a prayer partner. I have stood on the capitol steps in Washington, D.C. with five thousand participants of

Women's Aglow Fellowship, interceding for our nation and government. I have also stood in a Buenos Aires plaza with three times that many people, praying and doing spiritual warfare for Argentina. In Germany, Denmark, Belgium, and Holland, I have joined believers to pray for those not yet reached with the gospel.

God has recently given me a new assignment: to zero in on a few young Bible school graduates who are headed for full-time ministry in the U.S. and at least six other nations. I know them all personally and have posted their photos on my prayer board above my kitchen sink as a daily prayer reminder.

Commissioned by Jesus and empowered by the Holy Spirit to do battle, this young "Joshua army"—with Bible school training and foreign language skills—will go places and do exploits I can only dream about. Yet I have a part in their ministries through prayer and intercession.

I continue to pray for my own children along with my "spiritual kids" around the world: Quinett, Keith and Dana, Sherry and Kim, Gregory, my two Davids, two Eugenes, Aaron, Mark, Charlie, Jon, Chris, Daniel, Jerry, Debbie, and Sharona. May every one of them make a difference in bringing people into God's kingdom.

Each of us—you and I included—holds a sphere of influence and a certain set of friends that no one else has. God puts them in our path for his divine purposes. One of those is to pray for one another.

Ask God for your prayer assignment and don't give up! The only way we lose the battle is to quit. In times of weariness and discouragment we must refocus on our Commander, Jesus Christ, and draw our strength from him. He is a mighty warrior!

—Quin Sherrer
Dallas, Texas

To write to either author:

Quinn Sherrer
P.O. Box 25433
Colorado Springs, CO 80936

Ruthanne Garlock
P.O. Box 226048
Dallas, TX 75222

Notes

ONE
Putting on the Armor

1. E.M. Bounds, *Winning the Invisible War* (Springdale, PA: Whitaker House, 1984), 24.
2. R. Arthur Mathews, *Born for Battle* (Robesonia, PA: OMF Books, 1978), 54.
3. William Gurnall, *The Christian in Complete Armour*, Vol. 1, abridged by Ruthanne Garlock, et al. (Edinburgh, Scotland and Carlisle, PA: Banner of Truth Trust, 1986), 59, 65, 82.

TWO
Taking Authority in the Name of Jesus

1. W.E. Vine, *Vine's Expository Dictionary of New Testament Words* (Old Tappan, NJ: Fleming H. Revell, 1981), 89.
2. Dean Sherman, *Spiritual Warfare for Every Christian* (Seattle, WA: Frontline Communications, 1990), 111. Used by permission of the author.
3. Sherman, 123.
4. J. Oswald Sanders, *Effective Prayer* (Singapore: OMF Books, 1961), 19.

THREE
The Power of the Blood of Jesus

1. G. Campbell Morgan, *The Teaching of Christ* (Old Tappan, NJ: Fleming H. Revell Co.), 254.
2. H.A. Maxwell Whyte, *The Power of the Blood* (Springdale, PA: Whitaker House, 1973), 44, 78.
3. Mathews, 63.

FOUR
The Power of the Word of God

1. William Gurnall, *The Christian in Complete Armour*, Vol. 3, abridged by Ruthanne Garlock, et al. (Edinburgh, Scotland and Carlisle, PA: Banner of Truth Trust, 1989), 244, 245, 247.

2. Roy Hicks, Sr., "Faith's Confession of God's Word" in the *Spirit-Filled Life Bible* (NKJV), Jack W. Hayford, gen. ed. (Nashville, TN: Thomas Nelson Publishers, 1991), 1876.

FIVE
The Weapon of Praise

1. A.W. Tozer, *The Knowledge of the Holy* (San Francisco: Harper & Row, 1964), 102.
2. Jack Taylor, *The Hallelujah Factor* (Nashville, TN: Broadman Press, 1983), 31, 33.

SIX
Agreement Brings Boldness

1. Jack Hayford, *Prayer Is Invading the Impossible* (New York: Ballantine Books, 1983), 50-51.
2. Thomas B. White, *The Believer's Guide to Spiritual Warfare* (Ann Arbor, MI: Servant Publications, 1990), 155.

SEVEN
Other Strategies for Battle

1. Arthur Wallis, *God's Chosen Fast* (Fort Washington, PA: Christian Literature Crusade, 1968), 41, 42.
2. Dick Eastman, "Advancing in Spiritual Warfare" in the *Spirit-Filled Life Bible* (NKJV), Jack W. Hayford, gen. ed., 865.
3. Gwen Shaw, *God's End-Time Battle Plan* (Jasper, AR: Engeltal Press, 1984), 107.

EIGHT
Assured of Victory

1. Mathews, *Born for Battle*, 26-28.
2. William Gurnall, *The Christian in Complete Armour*, Vol. 3, 127.

NINE
Assurance of Salvation

1. T.W. Wilson quoted in *Topical Encyclopedia of Living Quotations*, Sherwood Wirt and Kersten Beckstrom, eds. (Minneapolis, MN: Bethany House, 1982), 11.

TEN
Overcoming Depression and Burnout

1. Archibald D. Hart, Ph.D., *Coping with Depression in the Ministry and Other Helping Professions* (Waco, TX: Word Books, 1984), 4, 5.
2. Mrs. Howard Taylor, *Behind the Ranges* (London: OMF Books, 1944), 90-91.

ELEVEN
Freedom from Anxiety and Fear

1. D. James Kennedy, *Turn It to Gold* (Ann Arbor, MI: Servant Publications, 1991), 83, 84.

TWELVE
Freedom from Guilt

1. Dr. Diane Mandt Langberg, *Feeling Good, Feeling Bad* (Ann Arbor, MI: Servant Publications, 1991), 192, 193.
2. Edwin Louis Cole, *Maximized Manhood* (Springdale, PA: Whitaker House, 1982), 118, 120.

THIRTEEN
Overcoming Grief and Disappointment

1. Alfred Ells, *One Way Relationships* (Nashville, TN: Thomas Nelson, 1990), 114.
2. From notes of a seminar presentation by H. Dale Wright, "Grief in Dysfunctional Families," given at Midwestern Baptist Theological Seminary, Kansas City, Missouri, April 28, 1988.
3. Ells, 124, 125.

FOURTEEN
Regaining Self-Esteem

1. Langberg, 152.

FIFTEEN
Warfare for Your Marriage and Broken Relationships

1. Dr. Archibald D. Hart, *Healing Life's Hidden Addictions* (Ann Arbor, MI: Servant Publications, 1990), 164.
2. Quin Sherrer and Ruthanne Garlock, *How to Pray for Your Family and Friends* (Ann Arbor, MI: Servant Publications, 1990), 52.

SEVENTEEN
Fighting against Childlessness or Abortion

1. Gary L. Bauer, Vantage Point column, "Deceptive Arguments," Focus on the Family *Citizen* magazine, Colorado Springs, CO, March 16, 1992, 16.
2. Penny Lea, "Rachel Weeping," 1987 pamphlet by I Believe in Life, P. O. Box 34077, Pensacola, FL 32507.

EIGHTEEN
Victorious and Single

1. Michael Cavanaugh, *God's Call to the Single Adult* (Springdale, PA: Whitaker House, 1986), 81.
2. Michael Cavanaugh, founder of Mobilized to Serve, speaking on "You

Are Complete in Him" to student body at Christ for the Nations Institute, Dallas, Texas, March 30, 1992. (To contact this ministry, write: Mobilized to Serve, Elim Fellowship, 7245 College Street, Lima, NY 14485.)
3. Ray Mossholder, *Singles Plus: The Bible and Single Life* (Lake Mary, FL: Creation House, 1991), 62.
4. Mossholder, 123.
5. Dr. Archibald D. Hart, *Healing Adult Children of Divorce,* (Ann Arbor, MI: Servant Publications, 1991), 179-80.

NINETEEN
Material Provision

1. E.W. Bullinger, *The Companion Bible* (Grand Rapids: Zondervan Bible Publishers, 1964), appendix 170.1.
2. Harold Lindsell, Ph.D., *Lindsell Study Bible, The Living Bible Paraphrased* (Wheaton, IL: Tyndale House, 1980), 1052.

TWENTY
Protection and Security

1. White, 105.

TWENTY-ONE
Healing

1. Sherman, 147-48.

TWENTY-TWO
Deliverance

1. Bounds, 33.
2. Sherman, 85.
3. C. Peter Wagner, *Warfare Prayer* (Ventura, CA: Regal Books, 1991), 16-18.

TWENTY-THREE
Intercession for Others

1. *New Comprehensive Shilo English Hebrew Dictionary,* compiled by Zevi Scharfstein (New York: Shilo Publishing House, 1973), 295-96.
2. Eastman, in the *Spirit-Filled Life Bible* (NKJV), Hayford, gen. ed., 1108.
3. Judson Cornwall, *Praying the Scriptures* (Lake Mary, FL: Creation House, 1990), 212-13.

TWENTY-FOUR
Battling against Deception

1. *The E.W. Bullinger Companion Bible* (Grand Rapids, MI: Zondervan, 1964), appendix 19, 25.

TWENTY-SIX
Praying for Spiritual Leaders

1. William Gurnall, *The Christian in Complete Armour,* Vol. 1, 84.
2. C. Peter Wagner, *Prayer Shield* (Ventura, CA: Regal Books, 1992), 50 (reference form manuscript version). Used with permission of Dr. Wagner.
3. Wagner, 49-56 (reference from manuscript version).
4. Cindy Jacobs, *Possessing the Gates of the Enemy* (Tarrytown, NY: Chosen Books, 1991), 126-28.
5. Elizabeth Alves, *Prayer Manual* (Intercessors International, P.O. Box 390, Bulverde, TX 78163; 1987), 129.
6. Wagner, 48 (reference from manuscript version).

TWENTY-SEVEN
Mobilizing Prayer Groups

1. Jamie Buckingham, *The Nazarene* (Ann Arbor, MI: Servant Publications, 1991), 87-89.
2. Cindy Jacobs, "Mobilizing For Strategic Prayer," *Intercessor's Digest,* published by Issachar Frontier Missions Strategies, P.O. Box 6788, Lynnwood, WA 98036, 1991.
3. Jacobs, *Possessing the Gates of the Enemy,* 202-203.
4. Jacobs, *Possessing the Gates of the Enemy,* 203-205.
5. A good source of information for setting up your church's intercessory prayer group is found in The Power of Church Intercession, a pamphlet published by Breakthrough, The Catherine Marshall Center, Lincoln, VA 22078, available for $1.00.

TWENTY-EIGHT
Praying for Your Neighborhood, City, and Nation

1. C. Peter Wagner & F. Douglas Pennoyer, eds., *Wrestling with Dark Angels* (Ventura, CA: Regal Books, 1990), 76-77.
2. F.F. Bruce, *The Epistle to the Hebrews* (Grand Rapids, MI: Wm. B. Eerdmans, 1964), 33.
3. John Dawson, *Taking Our Cities for God* (Lake Mary, FL: Creation House, 1989), 115-16.
4. Barbara James, *Intercession: A Call to Women* (Oklahoma City, OK: Pentecostal Holiness Church Headquarters, 1989), 26.
5. Adapted from the seminar tape,"How to Pray for Your City," by Dr. C. Peter Wagner [CEFI] and the book, *Taking Our Cities for God* by John Dawson, Creation House. Chart published by Fuller Evangelistic Association Newsletter, P.O. Box 91990, Pasadena, CA, April 1992, 2.

Other Books of Interest from Servant Publications

A Woman's Guide to Spiritual Warfare
Quin Sherrer with Ruthanne Garlock

Women everywhere face battles that threaten to overwhelm them and those they love. What can women do in the face of such monumental difficulties? *A Woman's Guide to Spiritual Warfare* shows how they can work with God to change the course of their lives and the lives of family and friends.

Quin Sherrer and Ruthanne Garlock help readers recognize the tremendous spiritual power God offers them to resist the enemy. **$8.99**

How to Pray for Your Family and Friends
Quin Sherrer with Ruthanne Garlock

How to Pray for Your Family and Friends is full of practical wisdom to help readers learn how to pray persistently and specifically, how to base their prayers on scriptural promises, and how to overcome barriers to effective prayer. Not only is this book full of inspiring illustrations of answered prayer, it actually contains specific prayers and practical instruction to apply to personal concerns. It will launch its readers into one of the most exciting adventures they will ever have—moving mountains with God. **$8.99**